# A Brush with Life

## The workhouse

The Thanet Union workhouse was a grim place, a bit like an open prison.

On the far left are the two workhouse blocks themselves. Mother lived and worked in one of these, in the laundry. I never knew which one. In the middle is what was later called the Asylum Block, where I was born.

At top right are lines of little shacks where some of the men lived. Many men, and some of the women, worked the surrounding fields, which belonged to local farmers. Over on the left you can see the pigs they looked after.

Along the bottom is a line of staff houses leading to the main administration block, with a bus-stop at the corner.

# A Brush with Life

Frank Sidney Smith
and John Man

Weidenfeld and Nicolson
London

First published in Great Britain in 1993 by
George Weidenfeld and Nicolson Ltd
Orion House, 5 Upper St Martin's Lane
London WC2H 9EA

British Library Cataloguing in Publication Data
A Catalogue record for this book is available from the
British Library

ISBN 0 297 83231 X

Paintings photographed by Geoffrey Goode

Designed by James Shurmer
Typeset in Horley Old Style by Selwood Systems Ltd
Printed and bound in Italy by L.E.G.O., Vicenza

# Contents

# A LIFE MADE WHOLE
## Foreword by John Man

FRANK SMITH opens windows onto many other countries where they do things differently. The past is one, childhood another. Then there are particular places, particular experiences, all made vivid by Frank's child-like vision, ready humour and crystal memory.

Here, for a start, are some intriguing byways of social history – workhouse, children's home, evacuation, farm labouring, army service, factory work. Frank speaks for ordinary people whose voices and talents remain largely unexpressed.

In particular, he records the last days of a workhouse, the Thanet Union, in Minster, East Kent, part of a miserable system of poor relief that had been in existence since 1834. The workhouse was the product of a grim dogma: that the poor, the unemployed, the destitute were always to be held responsible for their own misery. Moreover, since they were sustained by the rate-payers, they were in effect stealing from their fellows. The workhouses, of which there were many hundreds, provided work in exchange for wages. But they were also both a punishment and a deterrent. 'Our object', declared one of the early Poor Law Commissioners, 'is to establish a discipline so severe and repulsive as to make them [the workhouses] a terror to the poor.' In all but name, workhouses were prisons for those guilty of the crime of poverty. The Thanet Union, built in 1836, was as grim as any.

Fortunately, there were 'sentimentalists' enough to see that poverty had many causes, and to ensure that the system was not applied with equal rigour everywhere. Some poor – like the old and the infirm – were judged 'deserving'. As the vote was extended to men of the working class, pressure for change grew. In the 1890s toys and books were permitted into workhouses; committees of ladies were allowed to inspect; visitors could bring tea, milk and sugar; nurses could be employed. But the paupers – still mostly 'undeserving' – were stigmatized with a special uniform and did not have the right to vote. That right was granted only in 1918.

In 1905 a new commission condemned the 1834 system, pointing the way towards the modern welfare state. Old age pensions were introduced in 1909 (though there were still those who would have treated even the aged poor as criminals). Workhouse children received better care. The Manston Cottage Homes, where Frank spent his childhood, date from 1902.

It was not until 1929, though, that the workhouse system changed. 'The Union' came under the control of the local authority and was updated. In the 1930s it was mainly used for the care of the elderly (though Frank's mother remained). In 1939 it became a military hospital.

As a child, Frank saw the tail-end of this system. He is perhaps the only artist who thought it worth recording. His true purpose, though, is more fundamental, if less conscious. He has a restless personality, driven by a need to create. He uses his talent as others use talk, friends, written words – as a tool to achieve self-knowledge.

And self-healing. He never knew who his father was. His mother was largely absent. He was raised in an institution. His wife was schizophrenic and died from an officially administered overdose of lithium. His son was also schizophrenic, and committed suicide. These are burdens that could excuse bitterness and depression.

On the contrary: Frank seems strengthened by his struggle. That was what attracted me to him and his work. I was intrigued by the relationship between the two, between personality and its expression in art. Some people respond better to crisis than others; and some (not always the same people) cope better with the consequences. Both types are survivors. So is Frank.

Why? What traits ensure emotional balance under stress, and turn adversity to advantage? In Frank's case, part of the answer must lie in his sunny disposition and sturdy sense of individuality, and another part, surely, in his artistic temperament. The pictures reflect two traits shared by many survivors: an ability to feel (for trauma often numbs); and an ability to analyse, absorb and resolve those feelings, partly through humour. In effect, when he decided to tell his life-story through painting, Frank became his own untutored therapist.

Like many others, he found the business of painting itself therapeutic. It demands quiet, contemplation, the creation of one's own space. It rewards effort by revealing and developing hidden skills. It contributes to a sense of self-worth.

But mere effort, mere activity is not enough. 'Creativity' does not exist in the abstract. There must be something to express, and a means of expression – technical skill.

Frank's skill lies less in the simple, often raw style of his painting than in the choice of subject and the design. He focuses on the ordinary as well as on the obviously emotional, on children playing in a stream as well as on his mother's visit to the children's home or the death of his son. The viewpoints – the bird's-eye views, the rooms that zoom away into the middle distance, buildings that stand like theatrical flats, the removal of a wall, here a rangy landscape design, there an upright – are all carefully chosen to emphasize the subject.

Always he is meticulous about detail, not so much of the figures but of their surroundings. When he decided to paint his life, he accepted without question that he would return to as many places as possible to make sure he got it right. The people are defined by their surroundings, which have to be recorded as objectively as possible – 'If you can't do that, best forget about it.' He does not paint from imagination. He does not paint his dreams or play with abstractions or symbols. Emotion grows directly from setting and incident. It is in portraying this combination – emotion within an objective context – that healing lies.

# YEARS OF JOY AND SORROW
## Introduction by Frank Sidney Smith

I WAS BORN in the Thanet Union workhouse, but I was moved to the Children's Homes in Manston when I was still a baby, so I only remember the workhouse from later visits. My first memory was of the Children's Homes, when I was three or four. I was looking out of the iron railings, wondering what life was like on the outside.

I only discovered when I was eleven. Until then, I was raised in the Homes with my two brothers, Reg who is three years older than me, and Ray who is four years younger. There was no family life – we hardly saw anything of Mother and she never spoke about my father, nor much about the fathers of the other two. Sometimes Mother told me things about him, but they were always different things, to make sure I never found out the truth. Being in a home, with Mother in the workhouse and no family, sounds grim, but I had never known anything else, so I didn't expect better. Besides, the home was a well-run and caring place. We had a lot of fun, with trips to the seaside, and presents at Christmas.

I didn't know much about Mother. She had a sad and secretive life. She only told me bits and pieces. I do know she was a local girl. One of her grandfathers, Albert Emptage, had been famous as coxswain of the Margate lifeboat. He had helped save twenty-seven people when a passenger ship, the *Persian Empire*, was wrecked off Margate in 1897. The family must have fallen on hard times, because Mother was born in the workhouse in 1898. That was where she spent most of her early life, except when she sometimes went off to work in service.

It was this that made me wonder about my father. All I know for sure is that he was not the man my mother married, the Mr Smith after whom I was named. I never discovered when she married him. I never met him.

Not knowing who my real father was always nagged at me – it still does – and I have never stopped trying to find answers. There aren't many, but I have a few ideas. Mother worked once for a local bigwig in Ramsgate who later became a consul somewhere in Italy. He and his wife had had a deaf-and-dumb child, and the wife was always falling ill. She never had any other children. Mother was in the house a good deal, long enough for one of the other servants, Susan, to become her best friend, and long enough for her to learn sign language to communicate with the child. It may be that the man employed her to work and used her sexually as well. Perhaps when she got pregnant he sent her back to the workhouse to have the child – me – to avoid a scandal. Later, when he went to Italy, he took her along as a servant. She was there for a year, 1933–4.

What makes me think that man was my father is that he seems to have been an artist. When I revisited Margate as a grown-up, I went to see Susan – 'Auntie Susan', as she was to me. She gave me a book on figure-drawing that had once belonged to her master. And in the hall of the house I noticed a bust of a woman who looked very like my mother.

The war brought my childhood in the home to an end. As an evacuee, I spent happy years in the Midlands countryside. These times were full of new experiences. I hadn't had much to do with animals, so this was an education. I saw and did things that children don't experience much these days. Not many people have helped slaughter a bullock. It sounds gruesome, but that sort of thing was normal then. We got used to it.

Then it was back to Birmingham, with Mother and her new husband Henry. I had hoped for the family life I'd never had, but it was a terrible disappointment. Henry was a horrible man, bad-tempered, bad-mannered and violent. He often hit me. That was a real shock. I had never experienced violence before. Mother wasn't much help. When I started work, the two of them took all my wages and only gave me a shilling a week pocket money. I wasn't allowed to mix with other teenagers, and they kept me at home to do the odd jobs. The trouble was Mother never learned how to care for children, and she was too weak to stand up to Henry. I left.

Soon after, I was called up for National Service. As soon as I started, I signed on as a regular. A year in Palestine almost ended everything for me when I was wounded in the stomach by a sniper's bullet. Then it was to Korea with the Marines. That was when I started writing to Doris Palmer. Writing led to romance when we

Minnie Clara Smith in 1934

Albert Emptage, Minnie Clara Smith's grandfather

met, then marriage. There were strains right from the start because Doris had emotional problems. She had her first breakdown the day we'd planned for the wedding.

I might have known that was a sign of things to come, because both her parents were unstable. They came over from Australia to stay with us, thinking they might settle in England. But the change affected them. Her father couldn't stand the climate, her mother was a nag. He had a breakdown, then she did as well, attempting suicide by cutting her throat. Both went into mental hospital at the same time. The doctors saved her, and luckily they both got well enough to return to Australia.

I hoped the birth of our son Roger in 1958 would start a happy time. But Doris couldn't even leave hospital with him – she had another breakdown. She was so depressed that it was obvious she couldn't care for a baby. For weeks I had to look after Roger in the early morning and evening and work during the day, leaving him to the care of a neighbour. When Doris came home she was on the lithium tablets all the time, which kept her well enough to care for Roger. When she was well she was a marvellous mother, and I loved her deeply. But the same thing happened when our second son, Gregory, was born in 1961.

After Gregory was born, I was mother and father to the two little boys, with help while I was away working during the day. Doris did improve, but she never got completely better. Then gradually she declined. She would go red in the face, and talk a lot, and move her tongue in and out. A bit later she started giving things away, and keeping cupboards full of brown-paper bags. Things came to a head when she jumped out of bed one night, shouted 'Fire!' and began throwing things out of the window. After that, she started treatment in the mental hospital.

Roger and I saw her every day. One night Roger came back late and woke me to tell me Doris was worse. She was transferred from the mental hospital to a medical hospital, the East Birmingham. For two days she was in intensive care, then back on the wards. We went to see her every day for a week. She was a tragic sight, tranquillized on lithium. Her tongue was hanging out and she couldn't swallow. Slowly she slipped into a deep depression. Worst of all for me was that no one would tell me why. In the end she was on oxygen, in a coma. All the family came to see her – me, the two boys, Ray, Reg and Reg's wife. We left worried sick, but with no idea how bad she was.

She died late that night, without anyone telling me she was near death.

Still the hospital gave me no information. Only from the coroner did I learn the cause of death: lithium poisoning. She had been given too much over the previous two years. Many of her problems were caused by side-effects from the tablets. That discovery almost destroyed me. The hospital had said nothing about it. I had to do something, so I went to a solicitor.

It took almost ten years, but eventually the hospital settled out of court. They offered £1600. It was at least an admission of responsibility. I agreed, and felt justice had been done.

**Scraping the rice pudding dish**

Twice a week we had rice pudding. I loved it, especially the skin. As a treat, the house-mother let you scrape the dish out.

One day she said to me, 'Frank, you've been a good boy. You can scrape the dish today.' It was like a Christmas present. There was plenty of skin round the edges. She gave me a knife to scrape with, and a spoon, and I cut the skin around the edge, and it dropped into the bottom of the dish. You can see me spooning it up. Jack is eyeing me from across the kitchen – 'Lucky devil, Frank!' Slowly, to show how lovely it was, I put the spoon in my mouth, and felt the skin slip down into my belly. 'That *was* nice, house-mother!' I said.

Still, to this day, I like to eat the skin of rice pudding.

Roger never got over his mother's death. I'm sure that was what brought out his own schizophrenia. I recognized the symptoms – the depression, the wild talk – and managed to get him into hospital for treatment. They gave him largactil – he wouldn't take lithium – and electric shock therapy.

Then I discovered that he had been drinking heavily, making strange friends, hanging around in the local pub and taking drugs, mainly cannabis but also some cocaine and LSD. I couldn't stand him taking drugs, especially behind my back in my own house. I decided to find out where he was getting his supplies from. So I went to the pub, sat quietly and kept my eyes open. In the end I knew who his mates were, and knew what to look for. I contacted the police. They played along. I even had them search Roger's room, find drugs and lead him away in handcuffs. Imagine, my own son! But there seemed to be no other way to shock him out of it and make sure the house was clear. They let him go after twelve hours.

By now he was very ill, what with the schizophrenia, the treatment and his own drugs. He was in and out of hospital, staying with me a lot, but based in his own council flat when he was well enough.

Once he attacked me. We were on a bus, on the way to hospital. It was his birthday, his twenty-eighth. He wanted to get off and have a cigarette. I told him we had to go on to hospital. He set on me. I managed to pin him to the seat, but he kicked me in the stomach. A passenger called the police, and again he was arrested. He was sorry afterwards, because he was a loving son at heart, and went to hospital with me quietly. I bought him a pipe and some tobacco for his birthday.

It took a long time for my stomach to heal. I was in such pain that I went to the doctor. When I had an X-ray, I was very surprised to discover that I still had a bullet in me from the shooting incident in Palestine.

The beginning of the end for Roger came during another stay in hospital. For some reason he ran out into the road and got knocked over. He was unconscious for two hours. After that he seemed different, quieter but distant. Not till later did I discover that his mate, who lived near him, had committed suicide by cutting his wrists. That was what must have pushed him over the edge.

He came out of hospital, and for a month spent much of his time in my house, going to his own flat when he was well enough. One afternoon I came back from work to find some men waiting – plain-clothes police, I think. They told me terrible news: Roger had fallen from the balcony of his flat. I don't think it could have been an accident.

There are times when I wonder how I kept going. So many tears. I think perhaps it's because I always had to look after myself. I was never afraid to do what I thought was right.

In 1968, for instance, I was very moved by the fate of the Czech people during the Russian invasion. In fact, on the first anniversary of the invasion – 21 August – I laid a wreath at the war memorial in Birmingham. I made sure the papers reported what I was going to do, and asked for people to join me. A couple of English people did, and so did a few Czechs. It was something I was proud to do, never mind what people thought. I kept on laying a wreath every 21 August until 1989. I also made a wood-and-brass cross which I gave to the cathedral, with a plaque attached: 'Czechoslovakia, August 21 1968. The struggle for freedom, justice, truth and human dignity. The world shall remember.'

I've always been a bit like that. At work, I never had much time for the politics of the union. The union itself, the Amalgamated Engineering Union – that was another thing. I was loyal to the union. But not to the convenors and shop stewards who used it for their own political purposes. I noticed that when the companies closed factories down and we were supposed to fight the redundancies, it was the convenors and shop stewards who were the first to take redundancy money.

But I think the thing that really helped me most through the pain was the painting. I'd been doing bits and pieces for years, entering poster competitions and sketching at work. Then in 1976 I started going to night-school. At first I was just copying calendars. Then I thought there was no point in copying what someone else had done. I ought to be doing something of my own. That was when I decided to paint my life. I honestly think it was that work that kept me sane. All through the troubles with Doris and Roger, through union problems at work and then redundancy, the painting was something I could always go back to. There was always more work to be done. I felt I was achieving something. I was very proud when in 1981 I took O-Level Art, and got a Grade A. It was the first public exam I had ever done in my life.

Even in the middle of a time of sorrow you have to find some way of putting the sorrow to one side, and find a place where you can be yourself. For me, that place is a room with a canvas.

The plaque on a cross made by Smith to commemorate the Russian invasion of Czechoslovakia in 1968.

> ⊗CZECHOSLOVAKIA⊗
> AUGUST 21st 1968
> THE STRUGGLE FOR
> FREEDOM,
> JUSTICE, TRUTH
> AND
> HUMAN DIGNITY
>
> THE WORLD SHALL
> REMEMBER

### The infirmary

Destitute mothers were brought here, to the Asylum Block Infirmary, to have their babies. I was born on the top floor. The mothers left their babies there, and were allowed to visit them and take them outside. As Mother told me in later days, she was not allowed to breast-feed me. She had to work during the day, and was allowed little time to give me any love. Nurses fed us from bottles.

Mothers had to do all the laundry, heaving the heavy baskets down all those iron stairs and pushing them over to the workhouse. I remember all this from later, when I was recovering from pneumonia there. I remember the feeling of sadness – no smiling faces in the workhouse.

At eight or nine months the babies were moved to Manston Cottage Homes in Manston, a couple of miles away.

# WORKHOUSE CHILD

*Minster, Manston, Ramsgate and Margate*

1928–1939

**The chapel**

This is the other side of the infirmary, with the chapel on the left. The chapel meant a great deal to the unmarried mothers, because they had been forgotten by others outside for having babies out of wedlock. There was nothing else to turn to, so mothers took their babies to be christened there. I remember being taken there once when I was ill. It was small, plain, with rows of seats making a passage up to the altar.

## Smokers' corner

I saw this little alley when I came back to the workhouse later, when I was ill. It seemed odd to me, seeing all these men leaning against walls, and sitting, and smoking like chimneys. Mother told me they were the road-sweepers and gardeners and the men who unloaded the lorries. They seemed tired and sad.

**The boiler house**

I knew the boiler house from the outside. Mother used to push me past in my wheelchair when I was recovering.

'Why are all those men so dirty? Why do they look so tired?'

'If you worked all day long shovelling coal you'd look like them.'

I finally went into the boiler house when I went back to the workhouse as a grown-up. I spoke to a boilerman who said one of the boilers had been there since the 1930s, so it couldn't have changed much since I was a boy there.

**Mother in the laundry**

Mother told me what it was like in there – big laundry baskets, machines to wash the clothes and bed-linen from the workhouse and Children's Homes, tanks for hand-washing, mangles, ovens for drying the sheets, and big tables for ironing. Mother said the mangle used to give her a backache.

I used to imagine it all until I went back in 1976 and found diagrams in the library showing all the machinery. It made me happy to know I could get it right, and understand Mother's life better.

### The Children's Homes

The Homes were cottages specially built for raising children, about two miles from the workhouse. The school-age children were separated into groups, twelve boys or twelve girls in each cottage.

We had to be up at six-thirty, and be washed and dressed, with beds made and jobs done and inspected before leaving for school. 'Your bootlace, Frank!' House-mother would say. 'Do it up! Tom, that tie! Put it straight!' Then we'd line up in the cottage grounds, boys and girls in separate groups. Here it's the house-father who marches us off. He was superintendent of all the cottages. 'Right! March on!'

It was a lovely time, that five-minute walk to school, with all our chatter and laughter, and the sound of the birds singing in the trees above our heads, seeing outsiders waving to us. Then we were there, in time for the bell.

**The young children's house**

Before starting school I was in this little house for the smallest children with my younger brother, Ray. Later, after I had moved into the houses for bigger children, I used to visit him. Here I am when I was seven, and he was four. You can see some other little ones looking out of the window, hoping someone's coming to see them.

As I did, they will go on to No. 1 cottage when they are six or seven, boys and girls living in separate rooms. Later, the boys and girls will move into separate cottages, then at fourteen it'll be out into the world to work.

**My favourite toy**

In the house for older children, I remember playtime best of all. It was a big room, with a dark floor and a cupboard full of toys, which we all had to share. There were shouts and squeals of 'I want my toy back!' but the house-mother would come in and make us share properly. There was a big old rocking horse (that's my friend Tom riding it), and a cannon that fired a dead match right across the room, and a wind-up car.

My favourite was the humming-top. There I am in the middle. You pumped it and pumped it, and the harder you pumped the more the lovely music sounded.

I thought that room was so big when I was little, but when I went back to check details for the paintings, I found it was really small, and I wondered how we all fitted in.

23

1980 F. S. Smith

**Eating fat**

'You'll eat that fat, Frank!' the house-mother used to say, standing over me. I was always in trouble for not eating fat. Chew, chew, and still I couldn't swallow it. There I am, last at the table as usual.

'It's all gristle and fat. It'll make me sick.'

'You'll eat it, and you'll have nothing more till you do!'

The other boys are laughing, and I'm thinking: You can laugh – I'll get you afterwards.

'Swallow it, Frank. I'll not have you late for afternoon school.'

What they made cows out of then I don't know. I cried, but it did me no good. Once House-mother laid me flat on the table, face up, trying to force me to swallow.

So I swallowed, that great gob of gristly fat. More than once the whole lot came back up again.

**Playtime**

This was the time we all looked forward to. Playing outside by the visiting hall. Kicking balls, or throwing them against the wall. Boys dressing up as cowboys, girls as nurses. Hoops to smack with sticks to make them go, and yo-yos, shiny things painted in two colours. Sometimes we played jacks, throwing five stones in the air and seeing how many you could catch on the back of your hand.

For the crippled children – there were three or four of them – push-chairs were the thing. Old bone-shakers they were, but we loved to push them, with the crippled children shouting 'Faster! Faster!' as we pushed them around over drains and rough bits.

**Bed time**

Before getting into bed we would say our prayers. Sometimes the house-mother would tuck us in. Some boys wet their beds, so we had rubber under-sheets. If you wet your bed, you had to wash the sheets. I didn't like those rubber sheets – they made me sweat.

I remember after dark, when the moon came up, it shone in the window – no

curtains, of course – and we made shadows on the wall with our hands: a duck's head, a rabbit, a dog.

Silence would fall. Then a whisper: 'Hey, Frank, what's that noise?'

'Seagulls on the roof of number seven.'

'Shut up,' said Sydney, who called himself Chigwag – no one knew why. 'I want to sleep.'

*F. S. Smith 1980*

**Visiting day**

Parents could visit once every three or four weeks. To some it brought excitement, to others sadness because they had no mothers or fathers. Poor John, standing at the door, tears running down his face.

Here's Mother, with me, Ray and Reg, on the second bench back on the left, talking to us all at once. Mother's got Ray on her lap, and I'm reading a comic. Buck Jones and Desperate Dan were my favourites. I'm eating a sweet she brought, and in my pocket are a few more, saved for later. I'll share a few with the other boys back at the cottage.

It seemed we'd hardly talked at all before it was time for Mother to go. Hugs and kisses and cries: 'When will you come again, Mother? You *will* come and see us?'

Unknown to me, Mother found jobs away from the workhouse at times. How did she know when she could come again? Sometimes it was me waiting at the gates, and crying.

F.S. Smith 1978

**Boot cleaning**

House-mother was strict. She had to be. She had to make sure we all kept the cottage clean, washing up, wiping the surfaces, sweeping, dusting, cleaning our boots. If we were cheeky, or fought, or stole anything, we got extra work and less food. This time,

Tom has cheeked the house-mother, and she has set him to cleaning all twelve pairs of boots while she prepares some food at the kitchen table. When he's finished, she'll check they're all spick and span.

F. S. Smith 1979

**Bath night**

Friday night was bath night. It took so long for the kitchen range to get the water hot that it was six boys to a bath, each one coming in turn when his name was called, sometimes by the house-mothers, sometimes older boys.

Carbolic soap was the thing, and a good scrubbing down. How I screamed when the soap got in my eyes! If the older boys were washing us, they gave us a splash of cold water to finish off. That left me flabbergasted and shaking. Once they even pushed a flannel in my mouth to shut me up.

Then into a clean night-shirt and ready for bed, nice and warm again.

**Castor oil**

Friday was also castor oil day. We all hated it, being made to line up and take a spoonful of the oily liquid. Like the rest, I shuddered and muttered how horrible it was, and sometimes tried to pretend I wasn't there.

'Don't hide, Frank, I can see you. Sydney, come out from under the table, you stubborn boy.' Sydney – 'Chigwag' – was always hiding. Once he hid in the cupboard. 'Open wide ... There now, it's all gone.'

Down it went, faces twisted, all the other boys laughing. One good thing, at least House-mother gave us a sweet afterwards, unless you were naughty and didn't queue up properly. No sweet for Chigwag today, because he hid under the table to get away from the castor oil.

We never knew why they gave it to us.

**Classes**

In the village school, there was one big room with two classes going on at once. Very confusing!

Mr Pinder, the headmaster, loved to stand in front of the fire. No one else got a look in. Once his belt broke and his trousers fell down, and there he was in his long johns, and us all laughing till we were nearly sick.

As a matter of fact we were very well behaved usually. Mr Pinder was strict – cane for the older boys, a ruler on the back of the hand for younger ones if they played up. We didn't dare do more than nudge one of the girls or giggle now and then. So most of the children turned out well.

But I never was much good at reading and writing. Perhaps it was because I was pining for Mother. Or perhaps it was because my desk-mate was a village boy – one of the 'outsiders', as we called them – who smelled so horrible I couldn't concentrate. Mike, his name was. He never had a bath, and everyone called him 'Stinker'. That's us, me and Stinker, sitting together, unfortunately, the third row from the bottom of the picture, and the second row from the front.

Whatever the reason, it was often me stuck in the corner with the dunce's cap on.

F.S. Smith 1985

## Watching the thresher

Threshing days were something! Mr Ernest Philpott's farm was right opposite our school gates. In autumn, we watched the threshing from the playground. We loved the steam-engine, with its flapping drive-belt. Men pitchforked the corn from a cart into the thresher. I remember the dogs going after the rats, and I once saw a farmer stabbing a rat with a pitchfork.

It was a sad moment when the bell rang and we all had to go back into class, especially as we could still hear the chuff-chuff and flap-flap of the machine.

**Playtime at school**

Round the back of the school was where the girls and little ones played. We were round the front, to prevent us knocking the little ones over, but you could see them throwing balls, bowling hoops, skipping and playing leap-frog. To see the girls leap-frogging was a laugh, because they had to tuck their skirts into their bloomers.

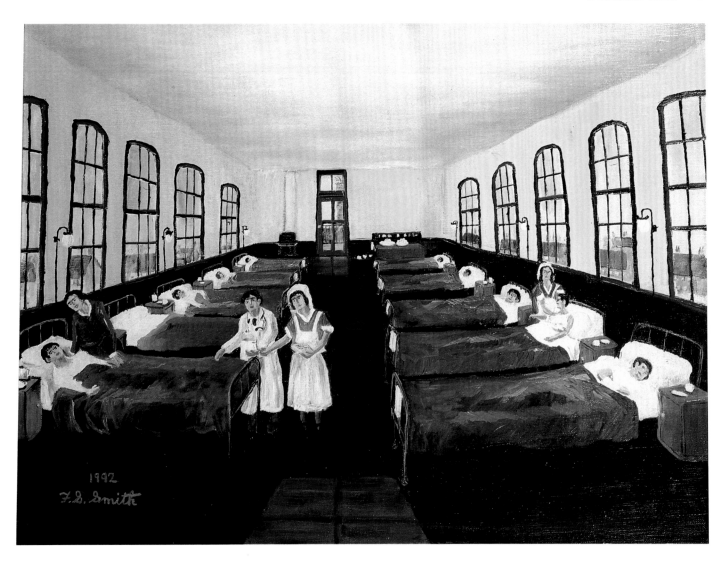

1992
F.S. Smith

**Sick with pneumonia**

When I was five or six, I fell very ill with pneumonia and almost died. I was rushed to the children's ward in the workhouse infirmary. I don't remember much, except a sort of haze with doctors and nurses in it. Mother was allowed to see me a lot.

This is the day I began to get better. Mother is leaning over me. I could see how much she loved me, even if she couldn't visit me much when I was well.

I remember the sun shining through the big windows, and the sky, and a single smoke-stack. Forty years later, when I went back, I saw the same smoke-stack – the one on the boiler house – and it brought it all back.

## Convalescing in the workhouse

As I got better, Mother began to take me out in a wheelchair. It was spring, and I began to get to know the workhouse and the people better.

In this picture that's me in the middle, with Mother pushing me. We are going past a First World War veteran with one leg, and another with his arm off at the elbow. A sad business, to fight for your country, lose a limb and end up in a workhouse.

On the left, Matron is giving orders to her staff. There's a mother with a new-born baby in a pram, and another convalescing child, a girl, being encouraged on to the grass by her mother.

F. S. Smith
1983

### The day the cameraman came

It was a special day, because we all had to have our hair cut and look smart. The boys from the Homes had a quick trim, and came out looking as if they had pudding-basins put on their heads to guide the scissors.

The photographer set up by a wall in the playground. You can see the place, over on the left. That's me waiting for my picture. The photographer is talking to the teacher, telling her how to organize the children. Then the photographer came back, put his head under the black cloth and said 'Watch the birdy!' A grin showing bunny-rabbit teeth – Click! – 'Next!' – and it was all over.

They gave the picture to Mother, and she treasured it until her death, when it came to me.

**Learning to darn**

House-mother would make us sit round in a circle so she could show us how to darn. It was important work, because we all had holes in our socks. We had needles, wool and a wooden 'mushroom' to keep the socks stretched taut for darning. Back and forth the needle went, often leaving big spaces until we learned to do it right.

'Ouch! I pricked myself!' Everyone would laugh.

'That'll teach you, Frank, for not paying attention.'

And it did, too. I learned to darn pretty well, and it came in useful in later life.

### The village shop

On Saturdays we were given a penny to buy
sweets in the village shop in Manston. We
walked over there in groups, happily
planning how we would spend our money.
The window was full of different sorts of
sweets.

'I'll have gob-stoppers!'

'I had gob-stoppers last week – liquorice
sticks today!'

'No, jujubes!'

So there we are, me with a gob-stopper
making my cheeks bulge, Freddy twisting
and tugging at his liquorice stick, others with
sweet cigarettes, pretending they're
smoking.

We were lucky to get that penny. Before
my time the children got nothing.

F.S. Smith 1981

**Manston church**

We went to church every Sunday. The house-mother walked us there, along the railings, past the farms and fields and trees. Opposite the church was a lovely war memorial, a stone cross surrounded by flowers in summer. The cross had the names of the villagers who had died in the 1914–18 war carved on it. Strangely enough, one of them was called Frank Smith.

**In church**

In those days the churches were full. I liked the feeling of warmth and security, not that I can remember many of the hymns or any of the sermons.

There was an old organ that had to be pumped by hand. It was my older brother Reg who did the pumping. Sometimes it would begin to fade, and the organist would mutter 'Faster, boy, faster!'

The Homes children sat at the back, the village people in the front, and there were all sorts in the choir, not forgetting some of the RAF from the airbase.

**Getting ready for Cubs**

Ironing night was also Cubs night. House-mother would iron all twelve uniforms, making sure we were smart, with nice green pullovers and caps, and a scarf with a leather clasp, and green tabs stuck on the socks.

The older boys were Scouts. Here am I as the house-mother finishes ironing, hoping to catch a glimpse of my older brother Reg through the window as he goes past to Scouts. She must have let me in as a treat, because the others are all in the dining-room, waving through the glass door to get my attention. You can see their shadows on the floor.

**The Scout hut**

Evening at the Scout hut was a good time, because the village boys and girls came as well. As Cubs, we learned to drill smartly, and do our best, and do good to others. We also learned how to make a camp-fire and watched the Scouts put up a bell-tent, with the Scout Master shouting at them as they held tight to the ropes and hammered in the pegs. 'There's my brother, Reg!' I would say proudly to anyone who would listen.

It was a cold place in winter, that hut.

F.S. Smith 1979

**Sharing sweets**

We were brought up to share, because some of the children had no fathers or mothers to bring them sweets. After Mother had gone, I would take one from the bag, then, once we were back in the cottage, the lucky ones like me would share out our sweets. Some got into a right mess, making their hands sticky and then making the doorknobs sticky.

## Caught in the act

It was my turn to fetch cocoa from the pantry. I looked round at the shelves, all well stocked – too much of a temptation for a hungry little boy. I knew it was wrong, but I couldn't help it. I looked at some of the tins. No, too hard to open. An apple? No, it would take too long to eat. Jam, that was the thing. Off came the lid, and in went my fingers.

'Frank! What are you doing?'
I jumped.
'Oh, Frank, you naughty boy.'
There I am, well and truly caught, waiting for punishment – a smack on the bottom, and straight to bed without any cocoa.

I never did anything like that again.

**The concert**

Every year there was a Christmas concert and panto in the hall, given by the RAF from the nearby base. One year, I remember, they did 'Jack and the Beanstalk'. The little ones and the crippled children were in front, and we all jumped when the beanstalk fell with a bang and a flash. Then the house-father, Mr Billings, played his piano-accordion, and we all joined in some carols, and the evening ended with cheers and claps.

48

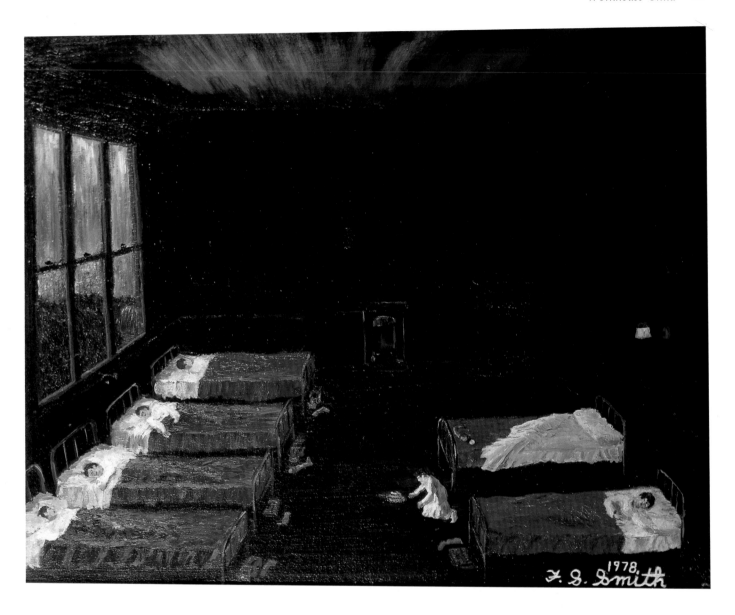

1978. *F. S. Smith*

**Christmas**

Christmas Eve was exciting because Father Christmas brought us all presents. We'd go to bed thrilled by the idea of a new fire-engine, or lead soldiers, or books, or dolls, or clothes for dressing up.

This Christmas, I'm first awake. What's Father Christmas brought me? Gosh – a tank! I've wound it up, and I'm watching it crawl across the room with sparks flying out of its turret. Soon, everyone else woke up and began playing with their toys.

There were two stockings for everyone. I discovered later the council made up one with a few toys. We hung out another of our own in which the house-mother put an apple and an orange.

*F. S. Smith*
*1981*

**Christmas tea**

We all helped decorate the room with paper bells and home-made paper-chains, all the links carefully cut out and stuck together with paste made out of flour and water. We set the table and brought in the food, going carefully with the cake and the trifle. Then we laid out crackers by each place. It all looked so nice and cosy, especially once or twice when it was snowy outside. A lot of our provisions, and I expect some of the toys, came from the RAF, so I've remembered them by painting in a plane landing at the aerodrome.

House-mother sat us down and said grace. Then the fun started, ending with the house-mother lighting the candles on the Christmas cake, and all blowing together when she called out, 'One, two, three – blow!'

### Heart-broken

Us boys loved kites, and I'll never forget the one I had. One afternoon, Freddy helped me get it flying high in the playground behind the Homes. We took turns running into the wind and letting out more and more string. When we reached the end of our string, we tied on more, and up it went, higher and higher.

We hadn't noticed that the wind was whipping up storm clouds. Suddenly, with a clap of thunder and a flash of lightning, it began to pour with rain. We pulled at the string with all our might, but we couldn't get the kite back down. Almost soaked, we tied the kite to the railings. Here I am in tears, crying all the way to the cottage.

Next morning, I looked out. The storm was over. But the line had broken and the kite was gone. All that was left was a short bit of string dangling from the railings.

## Summer storm

I liked lightning. If there was a
storm at night, those great flashes
of light and the roar of thunder
always got me out of bed. I wasn't
a sissy baby who screamed and hid
in cupboards, like one or two of the
others did.

'Gosh! Look at that!' I'd say,
staring at the flash and the shadows
on the wall.

'What's going on?' It was the
house-mother. Yes, she did come
round in storms to make sure we
weren't scared. 'Frank! Back into
bed! Go to sleep!'

But I lay awake, waiting for the
flashes, until the storm died away.

F.S. Smith 1982

### The boy who was knocked down

I had seen Harry walking or running past our gates most days for a few years, because I was for ever staring out of the windows. He was in the village school with us, but he was always there before us.

But this morning I wasn't looking. All I heard was a scream and a screech of brakes. House-mother and House-father ran outside, and there was Harry, lying in the road. This is them, carrying him to the first aid room, with our nurse leading them.

Soon an ambulance arrived and took him away to Ramsgate Hospital. Some time later, House-mother said he had died. Every morning after that, I felt sad not seeing him go by.

53

**Rupert the Bear**

As I got older, I moved to a different cottage. Pastimes here were more like hobbies. Here I am reading the *Rupert the Bear* annual which arrived every Christmas. We also had a castle with soldiers, and cannons that fired matchsticks. One boy is collecting a box of soldiers to play with. The third one is making plasticine models.

I loved the plasticine, squeezing it, rolling it, putting the parts together to make farmhouses and animals. I was never satisfied, always adding finishing touches that made the models that much nicer. I suppose that was the artist in me.

**Housework**

As we got older we had to do the housework. Saturday was scrubbing day, when everything had to be well done – polishing the floors, black-leading the grates, dusting, the toilets cleaned and disinfected, the kitchen spotless.

Here I am dusting the windowsill, looking out of the window, wishing I was running around outside. I remember the smell of the floor-polish, and the way you pushed the floor-polisher to and fro, to and fro, until suddenly the floor began to glow. The work didn't bother us – there were plenty of laughs and we were proud of ourselves afterwards.

**Me and Joan**

The playing field behind the cottages was always a happy place, especially in summer, playing ball, wrestling, picking hawthorn and nasturtium leaves to eat for fun.

I was fond of a girl called Joan. Here I am with her in the front of the picture. She is putting a buttercup under my chin and looking for the yellow reflection.

'Let's see if you like butter, Frank . . . Yes, you do, you do.'

And we're both laughing, because we didn't have butter in the Homes.

Other children are making daisy-chains. I loved doing that – gently sticking a pin through the stem, pulling through a second daisy, then another, then another, until you could join the ends into a chain, and turn it into a necklace. Joan looked very pretty with a daisy-chain round her neck.

56

**The snowman**

We all loved making snowmen, rolling the snow along the footpaths at the back of the cottages until they were balls big enough to be the body or head. Pieces of coal would make buttons, eyes and mouths. Then we would throw snowballs at the trees to make it fall, and chase the girls to put snow down their necks. Once they ganged up and chased me and shoved snow down my trousers. 'You rotten buggers!' I yelled, 'I'll get you for that!'

The fun didn't last long, because I had chilblains. I couldn't get rid of them, because we had no heating in the cottage except for the fire downstairs. Soon my woollen gloves were soaked and my chilblains hurt so much they made me cry. That's me on the left, sheltering by a wall and crying with pain.

1977 F. S. Smith

**Chicken-pox**

One day I woke not feeling too good. The nurse said it was chicken-pox and sent me to the sick-room. I was there all by myself for a week, with just a pot, a wash-bowl and a few toys. I spent the time looking out of the window, and lying in this den I made under the bed.

I'm day-dreaming, thinking: I wish the floor wasn't so blooming hard ... I wish I was better ... I wish someone else would get chicken-pox, because I'm fed up being alone.

### The pillow-fight

Sometimes, when we thought the house-mother was safe in her living quarters, this is what we got up to. Perhaps I started it, plonking a pillow on Bill while he was asleep. Then it was, 'Right, I'll get you, Smithy!' and we'd all be laughing and throwing and fighting, until r-r-i-p – I'd torn my night-shirt.

'What's all this noise?' That's the house-mother. 'Get in your beds this very minute! Frank, your night-shirt's torn, you naughty boy. Now, back to sleep! I'll talk to you all again in the morning!'

I was red in the face. We all went back to bed, and there was silence, until some voice said. 'It's all your fault, Smith. Now we'll all get extra work.'

Coronation day, 1937

(*previous page*)

## Coronation day, 1937

It was May, but cloudy and a bit rainy. We are with masses of other children in the Wellington Crescent Gardens for a march to the sea-front promenade. I'm somewhere on the left, with all the rest of the Scouts, Cubs and Brownies, all in our uniforms. A Salvation Army band is playing on the bandstand, and all the different villages have their own banners.

After that we marched off, with the band playing and people cheering. At the promenade guns fired a salute, which made us jump. Then they gave us a tin of chocolate with the new king, George VI, and the Queen on it, and sandwiches, and lemonade.

What a day! We were all so happy, never mind the rain.

## Coach trips

Sometimes we went on trips to Margate, Ramsgate and Broadstairs in East Kent coaches. I loved those coaches, the big, shiny body and the smell of leather and polish inside. Here are the driver and the house-mother wondering how to get a crippled boy inside. I'm looking out of the cottage window, waiting for the order to get in.

It was mostly in summer that we went on trips, and I loved rolling along through the beautiful green Kent countryside – the villages, the neat fields, the apple orchards and the hop-gardens.

**The rock shop**

I can't remember if this is Ramsgate or Margate, but anyway the shops were like magic to us. Mouth organs, some of them with a push button. Small harps you played with the mouth. Toys and seaside things, and 'Look! Look!' – here we are at a shop which sells only sticks of rock. There's a machine in the back pushing out the rock, with the name of the town written right the way through it.

'Boys, I'll buy you all one.'
'Oh, thanks, House-father!'
Over the other side of the street is a fish-cart selling cockles and mussels. I remember that, because my mother told me that my great-grandfather was the coxswain of the Margate lifeboat, and he sold cockles and mussels too.

1978
F. S. Smith

**A day at the beach**

In summer we all looked forward to our days at the seaside. East Kent coaches drove us to Margate. We all had our buckets and spades and a packed lunch. On the beach, we were kept in groups. Here we are lining up for a picture taken by House-mother with an old box camera.

The older ones went swimming, but the younger ones were only allowed to paddle. We had galoshes, funnily enough, to protect our feet from rocks and sharp shells when we paddled. The beach-man would give the house-mother a deckchair, and we would take off our shirts, boots and socks and set about building sandcastles and sand-cars.

Once when I was digging I found a treasure – a whole lot of lead soldiers buried by the tide, left by some other children who had been playing there. When I think of that find, I can still feel the joy of it.

## Margate dreamland

Two or three times a year we went to the fairground. We were all given candy-floss and allowed turns on anything but the big dipper, which House-father said was too frightening.

I liked the caterpillar best. A penny a go. You sat in a seat, and the wheels started to roll, up and down over little hills. Then the man pushed a lever, and a canvas hood came up over our heads and covered us in. In the darkness we went faster and faster, up and down, laughing as the wheels rattled. Sometimes little ones were scared, and cried until the hood went back and the caterpillar stopped. Then the laughs and smiles came back.

### The boy who ran away

This boy was an outsider, a new arrival. I can't remember his name. I just remember he disappeared one morning. We were told the police were out looking for him. I knew they'd catch him, because he was wearing the Homes' belt and tie, and everyone knew the colours.

It was after tea, and he was still on the run. Then a message came. A boy had been found crying on a long road.

Here he comes, a little boy sobbing his heart out, led by a policeman. 'I won't do it again, policeman,' I heard him say. He was given a meal and sent to bed.

Running away happened now and then, but it was always outsiders who couldn't understand what had happened to them. Those like me who had been born in the workhouse were so used to it we never thought of running away. The Homes was home to us.

### The last day

On 1 August 1939 my childhood ended. It was a terrible shock, because I never knew anything about the war coming. All I knew was that it was a really hot day. We had an old radio, but didn't listen to it much because it was so crackly. First thing I knew was when House-mother stopped me going for inspection before school.

'No school today, Frank,' said House-mother.

'Why?'

'I don't know.'

Then Mr Billings, the house-father, came in with two men. One of them said, 'Smith, you might be leaving.'

I still didn't know what was going on. I burst out crying, and shouting, 'I don't want to go! I don't want to go!' I cried so much they sent me up to my bedroom to wait. There I am, watching the others go off to school, wondering what was happening.

### Last time in the workhouse

Next thing, House-father took me and my brothers in the bus to the workhouse. We sat in a waiting room. I was still crying. The waiting room looked morbid – all those green tiles on the walls and passages. A man and a woman came in, then Mother and a matron. Mother had a suitcase.

Much later, I understood what was happening. We were being evacuated because Manston airbase might be bombed. The man and the woman were called Jesson. They were from Birmingham, and they had signed up to take us on. They had driven all the way down from Birmingham to fetch us.

There was some kind of argument between Mother and Matron. I heard Matron say: 'Minnie, you go now, and don't you ever come back.'

Then I knew this was goodbye to the workhouse and the Homes.

Mother picked up her suitcase.

'Time to go, boys,' she said.

**Goodbye to Manston**

This is my last view of the workhouse. We're getting into the Jessons' car. Matron is in the doorway. Three workhouse people are standing on the corner, by the bus-stop, with the timetable on the wall. They have come to say goodbye to Mother. House-father is standing by the car to see us in.

'Get in the car, Frank.'

I said goodbye to House-father and started crying again, and cried all the way past the workhouse, where Mother's friends were waving, and through Manston village, away from the friends I never even said goodbye to, off to Birmingham and a new life.

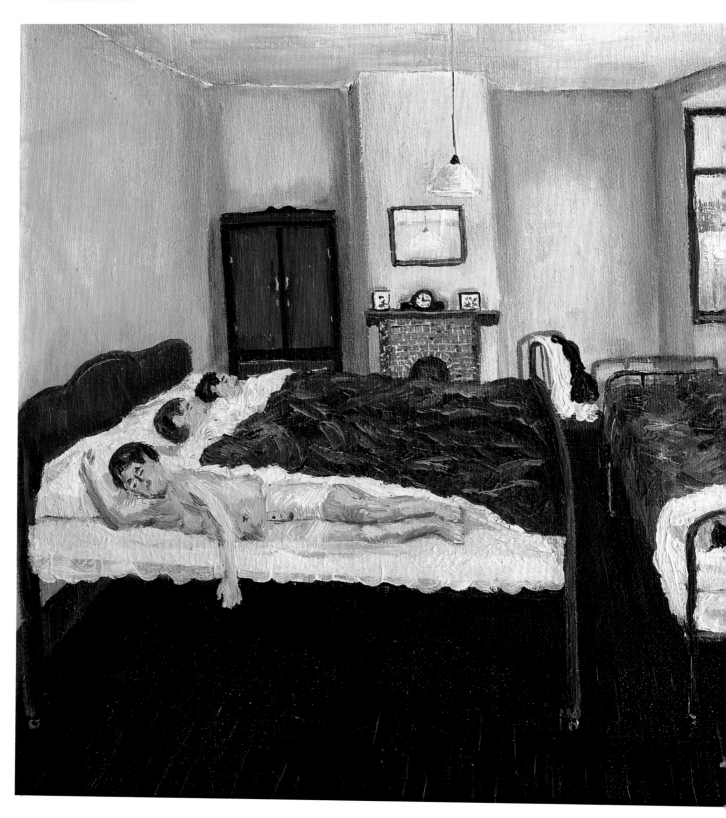

# THE WAR YEARS
## *Birmingham and Tanworth-in-Arden*
## 1939 – 1944

**First night in Birmingham**

After hours and hours, we arrived at the Jessons' house.
A hot dinner, a wash, then into bed, all of us crammed into
the front room. Mother and Ray in one small bed,
Reg and the Jessons' son Cyril and me in a double bed.
Cyril twisted and turned all night, until I was left
like this, freezing with no bedclothes.
It turned out the Jessons had just taken us in temporarily,
until Mother got a job. They couldn't really
afford to keep us. But Mother went back into service,
earning her keep but only getting a pound a
week – not enough.
Little Ray went first, sent off to a Dr Barnardo's home.
Then he was fostered through the rest of the war.
We'd only been there a few weeks when Mrs Jesson
packed our things, marched Reg and me through
the rain to the house where Mother worked,
shouted at her, 'You can have your bloody kids!'
and stormed off.

### The cruel coalman

Mother knew one other family in Birmingham. Mother's employers, the Newtons, made the arrangements. So we were taken in by Mr and Mrs Baker, at number 54, Golden Hillock Road. Somehow Mother knew Mr Baker from years before down in Ramsgate. It seemed like we'd be there for a long time. It was September now, and I began school.

One day out in the road I was watching a horse pulling a heavy coal-cart. Near the crossroads the horse got stubborn and stopped, blocking the road. The coal-man began to lay into the horse with his whip. The horse reared up, and I felt sorry for it.

I was only eleven, but I got really cross with the man. 'Stop that! It's cruel!'

'Buzz off, you little bugger, or I'll put this whip round your backside.'

'Bully!'

The man raised his whip at me, and used bad language. I got frightened and ran back to the Bakers. Next time I looked, the cart had gone.

1982
F.S. Smith

## Falling in

At the Bakers' we loved playing in Small Heath Park, with its swings, roundabouts and see-saws. It also had a shallow, muddy duck pond where we sailed little boats. One day my boat began to float away. I reached and reached, until splash! There I am in the water, but holding the boat safely. I couldn't understand how it had happened, and shouted at the others for pushing me.

I was in a state. 'Look at you!' said Mrs Baker. 'Stinking with all that mud!' She sent me out in the garden to have a wash down before she let me in to put on new clothes.

Small Heath pond is all filled in now.

### The last to be taken

War was close now. Again, the children had to be evacuated, being taken to a safe place in the country. All the schoolchildren were given gas masks and put on a train. This was when I was split up from my older brother Reg. He stayed behind at the Bakers because he was fourteen, and could work. Mother was in service again. She came to the station and I waved goodbye, crying, not knowing when I would see her again.

After a while, the train stopped. 'Wood End station! All out!' A man walked us over a bridge to a bus which took us to a schoolhouse. We were in Tanworth-in-Arden, ten miles south of Birmingham.

Into the schoolhouse we went. Grown-ups came and started to take the children. 'I'll have this one,' I heard people say, or 'I can take two.' The man ticked them off as they went. I went all solemn, and hid at the back. I never did like to push myself forward. In the end there were only two of us left, me and a boy called John Hall, and no more grown-ups.

At that moment, a little old lady came in and said, 'I'll take these two, then.' The man ticked us off, and the old lady led us out. Here she is holding our hands and leading us away from the school. I felt a glow of happiness come over me. I knew I had a new home, with someone I liked already.

F.S.Smith 1986

**Mrs Tibbles' cottage**

The lady's name was Mrs Tibbles. Dear Mrs Tibbles. She would remain an auntie to me until the day she died. She lived with her husband in this lovely cottage which was hundreds of years old. It had a roof that came down low at the back over the kitchen. The WC was outside. I noticed they had chickens, a goose and a pig.

Mrs Tibbles made us welcome with some tea, and I soon lost my shyness. Then she took us up little twisty stairs, through doors with wooden catches into a bedroom with a low ceiling. It was lovely.

Soon we were at home, playing with other children who lived nearby. Here we are playing 'Shoot the Germans' with rough wooden guns painted with creosote. That's me behind the fence, shooting at John Hall, Brian Higgins and Malcolm Broom. Once it would have been 'cowboys and Indians', but we knew all about the Germans and the coming war now.

### Hot bath in the cold parlour

That winter was really cold, so having a bath in what we called the parlour was an experience to remember. There was a pump in the kitchen next door which drew icy water from a well. Mrs Tibbles heated the water on the stove and poured it into this metal bath. A smelly, smoky paraffin stove was all the heat in the room. There's Mrs Tibbles, getting ready to give me a good scrub.

Perhaps because of the cold, or because everything was so new, I remember everything about that room – the side of pig on the wall, a chicken that had to be killed because it kept laying eggs in the bushes, a rabbit ready to go in the pot, pots and pans, and eggs and vegetables.

**Mr Tibbles' workroom**

Mr Tibbles was a tailor. It was odd – he always worked cross-legged on the table. Here he is making a pair of farmer's corduroy riding britches.

Mr Tibbles was an air-raid warden. He had a tin hat with ARP on it, for Air Raid Precautions. You can see it hanging on the wall with his gas mask. He had to make sure the village was all blacked out at night, so that the German pilots wouldn't know there were houses below. All the houses, like ours, had heavy curtains or blinds, and windows covered with sticky tape to stop the glass flying about in case a bomb struck.

**Bombing raid**

We were out in the country, so we didn't have any air-raid shelters. But the bombs seemed close when the Germans bombed Birmingham and Coventry. When there was a raid on, Auntie got us up and took us into the cupboard under the stairs. Once a cluster of bombs landed nearby. One of them dropped just two hundred yards from us. There was this great crash, and we were very frightened. I remember waiting by the light of one candle for the raid to finish, praying hard to God to keep us safe.

**Giving the pig an apple**

I looked after the pig. Even if she did stink a bit in summer, with the mess and flies, I learned that pigs are just as responsive and intelligent as dogs. They can be loving, kind and mischievous. She would snort at me, and nibble my leg or my bottom, and steal my broom. She loved having new straw put down for her, and would scream blue murder when I brought her food. As you can see, though, she was happy to take an apple from me.

**Washing in the kitchen**

The pump was in the kitchen next to the sink, so that was where we washed, in cold water. But at least the cottage had electricity, so Mrs Tibbles had an electric stove to cook on. Here she's taking a cake out of the oven while we wash. Probably she's telling off Peter, the dog, for taking a piece of my clothing: 'Peter! You naughty dog! Get into your bed!'

## The goose that died

One morning I went to let the hens
and the goose out. First came the
hens, clucking and scratching. Then
I expected the goose. But she didn't
get up. There she lay, in her nest.
I touched her. No response. I poked
her. Still nothing. Then I realized:
she was dead. Here I am carrying
her out, in tears.

'She's dead, Uncle,' I said to Mr
Tibbles.

'That she is, Frank. But she's still
warm.'

'Shall we bury her?'

'Bit of a waste, to bury her. I'll
bleed her, and you can pluck her
feathers. Then we'll eat her.'

'Eat her?'

'That's what she would have
wanted.'

Still crying, I did as I was told.
Then Mr Tibbles cleaned the
corpse.

'Rat poison,' he said. 'She ate rat
poison.'

'If we eat her, will we die?'

'No, Frank, it'll be all right.'

So Mrs Tibbles put her in the
oven, and we ate her the very next
day.

## Tanworth church choir

The Tibbles always went to church every Sunday, and we went too. Mrs Tibbles suggested to the Vicar that he put me in the choir – me, who had never tried singing in my life. I couldn't even read the hymns very well. But I thought I'd have a go.

Well, I felt very proud, smartly dressed in a black-and-white vestment, especially when the BBC came to broadcast a service. I sang as well as I could, but not knowing the words or the tunes, I was always a bit behind the others. I wasn't too surprised when after a couple of weeks the Vicar said perhaps it wasn't such a good idea after all. That was the end of my singing career.

**Emptying the lavatory buckets**

Friday was the day for emptying
the village lavatories. By then the
outhouse stank. We didn't have
toilet paper – we had to use
newspaper. Nothing would stop the
flies buzzing round your bottom.
So it was a good thing the men came
round every week.

The man is carrying the lavatory
pail to the lorry. I'm behind him,
holding my nose like grim death.
Then he'd bring the empty pail and
put it back under the wooden seat.
Auntie Tibbles would sprinkle
disinfectant, and everything would
be clean and fresh again.

### In the black-out

Black-out in a little village like
Tanworth was hard on old people.
I didn't mind – I had a lantern with
a candle in it that I liked to use if
I had to go out. At Christmas I had
been out for a walk up the road
with my lantern when I almost
bumped into an old lady.

'What's that? Who are you?'

'I'm Frank. I live with Mrs
Tibbles.'

'Oh, thank goodness. I can't see
very well.'

'Shall I take you home?'

'That is kind of you.'

She said she lived in one of the
almshouses nearby. We both knew
the way, but she was glad of the
company. You could hear rustles in
the bushes – probably a rabbit.

'Bit spooky, this lane,' I said.

'I'll say,' she laughed.

There are the almshouses, and
me showing the way with my
lantern. She thanked me a lot for
that. She didn't need to – I was
only too happy to do it.

### The slaughter of the pig

I'd been feeding the pig for months and got very fond of her, but the time had come. The side of pork hanging in the parlour when I arrived was all gone.

No food for her for twelve hours, never mind her screams. Then next day Mr Tibbles got a fire going, a table and a tin bath. Mr Simmonds the butcher came, with a man to help him.

I ran away as Mr Simmonds took his special gun over to the sty, to the screaming pig. Bang! The screaming stopped.

When I came back, the pig had been singed on the fire to get rid of the hairs, then scrubbed in the tin bath. I couldn't stop crying as I watched them cut her in half and rub salt on the two sides. They took one half for the butcher's shop. The other half Mr Tibbles hung up in the parlour.

**Slaughtering bullocks**

It wasn't only pigs that got slaughtered. Bullocks, too. That's Malcolm, Brian and me helping Mr Simmonds do the slaughtering. We had to hang on to the rope to hold each bullock as steady as we could. Mr Simmonds had this special humane gun, which fired a cylinder of metal into the bullock's head, then pulled the cylinder back into the barrel. Mr Simmonds is carrying a cane he used for sticking into the hole made

by the gun to finish the bullock off. Then he hung the carcass up with chains and pulleys, and started to cut it up. Sometimes it was me taking out the buckets of blood.

It was a terrible business but we got used to it. We all looked forward to being given the horns, plus a shilling each for our help.

**The sweet shop**

Mrs Barlow and her son ran the sweet shop. You only bought sweets once a month in wartime, because you had to hand over ration coupons. Auntie used to buy Fox's Glacier Mints for Uncle. For some reason, though, you could buy their treacle toffee without coupons.

The Barlows' ice-cream was something special. They made it out of custard powder, powdered milk, water and saccharine, because sugar was rationed. It had a bit of an odd taste, but it was popular. Everyone wanted ice-cream because the nearby village, Henley-in-Arden, used to have the best ice-cream in the country, they said, until the war started and the manufacturers closed down.

There's the dog Peter giving me his paw. Sadly, he went missing later. Mr Tibbles said he must have got shot by a farmer for chasing sheep or got caught in a rabbit-snare.

**Learning to swim**

In summer we loved going down to the stream and making a pool to swim in. One spot with trees hanging over it was just right for making a dam. Here are Malcolm, Gordon and I naked, piling branches, sticks, stones and mud across the stream to make it deeper.

What's that? Two girls laughing in the hedge!

'Oi! Scram!' I shouted, and we began to throw mud at them.

'I'm telling my mum on you, Smithy!'

'Go on then!' But we splashed into deeper water so they couldn't see us in the nude.

F.S. Smith 1982

**Playing soldiers**

With our home-made guns and me with my gas mask on, we're creeping up on Germans hiding behind the oak tree on the green. 'Bang! You're dead!' we shout, darting from wall to wall for cover. The Germans hid behind the church wall, but we out-manoeuvred them by running round the back of the pub, and shot them all dead.

We liked to pretend we were as good at fighting as the local Home Guard, who at first only had pitchforks and a few shotguns to fight off the invaders.

## Collecting wood

We had a cart made from old prams and bits of wood. It wasn't just fun, either. We used it to haul fallen branches from Mr Hicking's wood back to the village for firewood. Coming up Dousey Lane with a cartload of wood the wheel fell off, dropping half the load along the road. Here are Gordon, Malcolm and Brian collecting the logs while I jam the wheel back on. Push in the nail that holds the wheel on the axle, all covered in grease and mud, and off we go again. Pushing and heaving we got the cart to our houses and shared the wood out. Very useful it was, too, as coal was rationed.

F.S. Smith / 1985

**Trying to break the cane**

I used to say that I would break the headmaster's cane. I had more than my fair share of it. The headmaster, Mr Benson, was always on at me because I liked painting more than writing. (That's a poster of mine – 'Your Country Needs You' – on the wall at the far end.) It wasn't that I hated Mr Benson – I liked him really – but I hated that cane. Well, one day at school I got my chance.

It had been building up for some time. A few days before, I had been throwing paper, something we all did when Mr Benson was out of the class. This time, when he came back in, a girl raised her hand.

'Please, sir, Smith's been throwing paper at me.'

'Smith, come out here.' I went. 'I will not tolerate this sort of behaviour. Hold out your hand.'

I did as I was told, but I was too quick for Mr Benson, I jerked my hand aside, and he missed. That made him really cross.

'Give me your hand.'

This time he held it, and hit me fair and square on the palm. Ouch, it hurt.

A few days later I spilled my ink, and Mr Benson called me up again. As he raised the cane I suddenly felt angry, and snatched at it. You can see me here grabbing it with both hands, and bending it, trying to break it. Mr Benson and I wrestled for it together, ending up on the floor. When we got up, Mr Benson gave me a good hiding anyway.

### Tormenting the bull

A long driveway, the Mile Walk, led away below the village through fields to a farm. Down the walk was a field with a bull in it.

'Danger, Keep Out!' said the notice, but we decided to be brave little boys, because the bull had an iron mask on that stopped him seeing straight ahead, so he wouldn't charge. Besides, he was tied to a heavy weight. Brian, John, Gordon, Malcolm, Jeffrey and I crept up to him to shout at him and wave a red cloth.

But when we got to him, he raised his head. Up went the weight and he swung round.

'He's charging! Quick! The gate!' Here we are running and slipping through the mud.

'That was a close shave!' I'm saying.

Poor Jeffrey was on the other side of the bull, so he's running away across the field.

1984
Y. S. Smith

**Fetching spring water**

Most of the people in Tanworth had no drinking water. They had wells for washing, but real drinking water they got from the spring down the bottom of Tom Hill. That's John and me coming down the hill with buckets to get water for Auntie Tibbles. It was lovely water, pure and very cold. The village people used to say it made you live longer.

After the war, all the cottages had pipes put in and the spring was blocked. Most of the wells were covered in too.

### Mrs Bennett's front room

I had been with the Tibbles almost two years when Mr Tibbles got polio and died. Mrs Tibbles couldn't cope any more, so John Hall went back home and I moved to Mrs Bennett's. At first there was just me, Mrs Bennett and her son Phil.

I liked Mrs Bennett, and used to help her round the house. It was an old-fashioned place, without electricity. Here I am in my pyjamas, making toast for breakfast. I used to black-lead that big range, and polished the two five-inch shells that stood on either side. They were souvenirs of the First World War. Mr Bennett brought them home on leave, then went back and got killed. You can see pictures of him on the mantelpiece.

And I used to fetch a jug of cider for Mrs Bennett. She liked her cider, and got a bit tipsy at times.

**Having a bath at Mrs Bennett's**

Then, when I had been there only a couple of weeks, Mrs Bennett had a stroke, and for a while I had more work looking after her. I was there mostly on my own, with Mrs Bennett upstairs. It was so cold I had a bath in front of the fire. It was a peaceful time – black-out curtains drawn, fire stoked, paraffin lamp pumped up and burning bright, newspaper on the floor as a bath-mat. I'm washing with floor-soap, with little old bits stuck to it, because soap was such a job to get in wartime.

After a few days, Mrs Bennett's daughter Violet came with her two children Pamela and Peter.

## Almost seduced

Things changed a bit when Violet came with Pamela and Peter. Because there were soon other tenants as well, all three of them slept in my room, Violet and Pamela in the double bed and Peter in a single one. Pamela was twelve and Peter thirteen. They often got into bed together.

I was a little younger, so I went to bed first. One night when they came up, you can see what happened: Peter has me round the neck, and Pamela is pulling my pants off. I'm fighting like mad and she's saying, 'Hold him, Peter!' Then she grabbed my legs and the two of them lifted me on to the bed, and Pamela climbed on top of me.

I was only thirteen, but I knew enough to be really scared. What if Pamela got pregnant?

I fought and shouted, until suddenly there was a knock on the door – it was one of the other tenants telling us to shut up. Pamela and Peter didn't want trouble, so they let me go. They never bothered me again.

**Fighting at school**

It all happened because some silly girl told the teacher Peter and I had been flicking paper at her with an elastic band. Mr Benson gave us both a smack on the back of the head. I thought no more about it, but Peter did. As we were going to play, he spoke to Mr Benson. Probably he complained he had been hit harder than me, but I couldn't hear.

'What did you say to Mr Benson?' I asked. Next thing I knew – bang! A fist in the face. Peter trying to get even, I suppose. Anyway, I saw red and hit him back. Down we went, fighting like mad. There's Mr Benson coming out to break us up. He grabbed Peter, gave him a telling off and sent him in to wash.

Peter sulked all day, but it was his own fault. Being brought up in a home, I could look after myself, and he should have known it. I didn't go looking for fights, but I wasn't going to be pushed about.

**Throwing mice to the cats**

One summer evening while I was still at Mrs Bennett's I was walking past Mr Morgan's farm. He was guiding his cows across the road. He said something about all the work he had to do, so I asked: 'Mr Morgan, is there a job I could do?'

'Yes,' he said. 'You can feed the hens and pigs.'

Next evening I started. He took me to the stable where the chicken-food was kept.

'There you are,' he said. 'You'll find the food in a barrel.'

I opened the stable door, and two cats followed me in. They must have sensed something, because when I opened the barrel, good God, there were mice jumping about all over the place. I acted almost without thinking – catching them in my hands and throwing them to the cats.

**The cows at Morgan's Farm**

My next job was to learn how to milk the cows. First I had to get them into the shed. Then Mr Morgan showed me how to milk. I had a three-legged stool and a bucket. 'Now, Frank, squeeze, then pull gently, up and down, up and down.' It did feel funny getting hold of a cow's tits, sitting on the stool with the bucket between my knees. But I loved it when the warm milk came squirting out. Still, Mr Morgan had to finish off, because cows hold back some of their milk from strangers.

I was only there a week or two. He gave me two shillings and sixpence, which I thought was a lot until I started working for other people.

**Killing a rat**

That summer I was fourteen and left school. I started work gardening for Mr and Mrs Aston, for one pound ten shillings a week. My job was cleaning out and feeding the chickens and geese.

One day I went into the chicken house and found two dead. There was a rat in there. I grabbed a pitchfork and ran at it, scattering chickens and geese. I chased the rat into a corner, and stabbed it with the pitchfork. One squeak, and it was all over.

I was so proud of myself I took it to show Mrs Aston.

'Ah! Take it away! Take it away!'

I was a little hurt, and wandered off to get rid of it. Later, though, Mrs Aston gave me an extra sixpence for killing that rat.

**Fun in the stream**

Half-way along the Mile Walk it went under a bridge that carried the railway to Stratford-upon-Avon. A second arch went over a stream. We loved to play here in summer, the boys stripped to our pants, the girls with their frocks tucked into their knickers. We would lift stones to find beetles. Once I killed a weasel that had just killed a rabbit. A few times we saw snakes. They were probably only grass snakes, but we were too afraid to touch them.

**Picking up stones**

Farmers wanted stones removed from their hay fields, as the machines used to cut the hay were really low and if the blades were damaged by a stone it was almost impossible to get a spare. It was a job often done by prisoners-of-war and sometimes by the schoolchildren. We were told it was part of the war effort, and it was in a way because so many labourers were away with the forces. They said the same thing to get us planting vegetables or picking potatoes. It was all back-breaking work.

**The bomb crater**

One of the bombs that hit Tanworth landed in the sports field, making a huge hole. It was up one end, near a hay-rick. We turned both into fortifications, and then had a shoot-out with our wooden guns, throwing balls of clay for ammunition. 'Ow! That hurt!' I shouted as a clay ball landed right on my head. There were many bruises and lots of mud on our clothes, but we had great fun.

1989
F.B. Smith

**Taking the bull for a walk**

Soon after I left school at fourteen, I went to live with Mr and Mrs Holden at Aspley Heath, to work on Mr Johnson's farm. I stayed there for a year – a very happy time. I was a full-time worker now, earning thirty shillings a week and paying my way with the Holdens.

One of my jobs was to take the bull for a walk. He couldn't be left chained up inside all the time. First I had to get a clip on his nose-ring. His nose was so sensitive he would let me guide him out of the cowshed and along the track. But it wasn't easy. He would try to charge at hens and nibble the hay-rick and pull me off to where he thought the cows might be. Most of all he hated going back inside to be chained up again.

**Haymaking**

I loved this job – real man's work, with a machine and a horse, out in the fresh air, with the sweet smell of the hay. It was hard, too, having to raise and lower the tines in exactly the right place to rake the hay into straight lines. I remember being so happy that I sang at the top of my voice, bawling 'London bridge is falling down'.

The problem was that Mr Johnson only had a small farm, and he was poor and old-fashioned, so the machines were old, and so was the horse. She looks a bit rough here. That's partly because she's the first horse I ever painted. But she really was rough in real life because the harness was too small, and she developed a sore spot on her neck. In the end it got so bad she had to be put down.

**Taking a tumble**

Mr Johnson and I loaded the dried hay on to a cart pulled by Bill, the shire horse. I used to be on top, making sure the corners were built securely. It was difficult sometimes, because when you told Bill to gee-up he wouldn't lean and pull gently, but snatch at the cart as if he was about to go off at a gallop.

Here's what happened once. The bumpy field is all cleared, though you can still see where the hay had been lying in neat rows.

Bill has just jolted forward and the whole lot is sliding off the back, with me and the pitchfork mixed up with the hay. I'm fighting to get to the air, sneezing like mad.

Mr Johnson can't believe it. All that work for nothing!

He used terrible language sometimes. He went up to Bill and punched him right on the nose. 'Take that, you bastard!' he shouted at the horse.

**Cleaning the yard**

Work on a farm is never finished. The cowsheds to clean out, milk churns and milk coolers to be washed, and the floors to do, hay and cowcakes and mangles to be put out for the cows to eat, pigs and poultry to be fed, machinery to be maintained. Here I'm shovelling manure up from the yard.

On the left is the milk cart ready for loading. Once the horse bolted and threw the milk churns all over the road. I'll never forget seeing that white river pouring away into the ditches.

**Milking**

I was pretty good at milking now, sitting there on my stool with my head against the cow. This one cow had a terrible habit – she would kick the bucket over just when you had finished milking her, so you had to tie her back legs together.

That's the bull chained up alongside.

Sometimes he would frighten the daylights out of me, kicking out suddenly if a horse-fly bit him. When that happened, I just took my bucket and stool and jumped clear.

# CIVVY STREET

## *Birmingham*
## 1944–1946

### Home at last

Towards the end of the war Mother wrote to
the Holdens and asked me to go back to her place in
Birmingham. She had a new husband,
Henry Fessey. I was excited and happy – now
everything would be lovely, I thought.
This is my room in Mother's house. Not much to write
home about. Small window, green walls,
a grate, an old iron bed, and a gas light that wouldn't
light because the mantle was broken.
No wardrobe – I had to hang my clothes in Mother's
wardrobe. Also, my room was through her
bedroom – I had to knock whenever I went through.
Never mind – I would have put up with anything
just to be home.

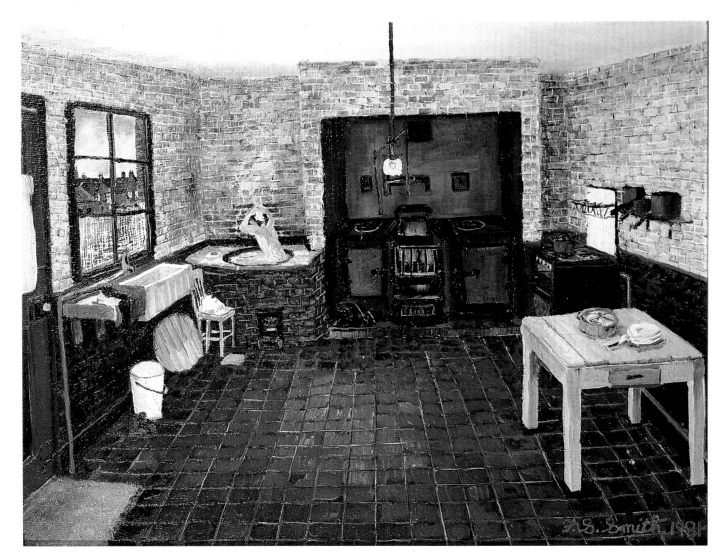

**Taking a bath in the boiler**

My hopes of happiness were soon destroyed. Mother and Henry were both tight with money. I'm sure Mother only asked me back because I was working and she could do with the money. She took all my wages, allowing me just a shilling a week.

Even though we didn't have a bathroom, and even though she and Henry went up the road to have baths in the public wash-house, I had to have my bath in the kitchen, in the boiler that was normally used for washing clothes. It was a business, stoking up the boiler, pouring the water in, then bailing it out afterwards down the sink. It was hard to climb into and far too small for me. And no privacy. I felt damned stupid.

**Mother's bedroom**

This would have been the view of Mother's bedroom if I could have removed the wall of my bedroom. Not much in it except a double bed, wardrobe, chest, a couple of chairs and two mats. That's Henry getting dressed. He was about fifty, and a moody, violent, lazy, foul-mouthed man. I disliked him from the start. I think Mother only married him because he had some cash for a deposit on the house. And filthy in his habits. He was always spilling the chamber-pot that stood under the bed.

### My stepfather punching me

I had my own work during the day – first farm-work, then at the rubber factory – but when I came home I had more jobs to do. Gardening, washing up, chopping wood, getting in the coal, black-leading grates, cleaning the toilet.

I wouldn't have minded, except it didn't make things any better. Mother would start moaning about the price of food – the eggs cost this, the lard cost that – and it would annoy Henry, and he would take it out on me. He would often just lash out at me, and fell me with a punch to the face. There was nothing I could do. He was six foot two and very strong.

In this picture I have just tried to escape outside and hide in the toilet. But he's caught me, and is laying into me.

After a few months I got so frightened I developed asthma and had to go to the doctor.

## A bitter decision

After I had been with Mother and Henry about a year, a neighbour noticed me crying outside. He knew what was going on of course. He said he knew someone who would have me to stay if I wanted.

I couldn't take any more. The home I had always wanted wasn't a home at all. There was no love here. So I said yes, please.

It took me another few days before I told Mother. Then I stood like this crying. I'll never forget that moment in that room, with the green walls and the red stripe and the plaster ornaments and the lino floor.

My last words to Mother were: 'I'll come and see you, but don't you ever ask me to come back.' I didn't tell her where I was going, either, because I didn't want them tracking me down.

1983
F.S.Smith

## The odd room

So I moved to Mrs Moore's, in Bournville, an area of Birmingham famous for chocolate, about three miles from Mother's. I was in this odd-looking room with the bath, which everyone used.

Being at Mrs Moore's brought me a lot of happiness. Mrs Moore was Irish, but she wasn't a religious person. She just had the kindest heart. She had heard about me from Mother's neighbour and just decided she had to do something.

I used to stand in front of that mirror doing arm-exercises, wishing I had muscles like Mr Moore, who worked in a foundry.

'You must be bloody barmy,' Mrs Moore used to say.

'Well, if I am, so are you. Only the barmy Irish would have a bathroom like this.'

She had three children. One of them, Peter, was still at home. Soon she looked on me as one of her own. She called me 'son' – still does, because she's still going strong in her late seventies.

**Peter and the bugs**

The local cinema, the Savoy, was known as the 'bug house', which it was. Once, after Peter came back, Mrs Moore saw him scratching.

'Son, you've brought bloody fleas back with you. Get them clothes off at once!' The hunt started. Shirt off, trousers off, down to vest and pants. That's where the fleas would be, hiding in the wrinkles and seams.

Mr Moore is in the chair, laughing, as Mrs Moore and I hold Peter's vest and pants to the fire. Mrs Moore is saying, 'Frank, you watch these buggers jump towards the heat.'

They did too. Pop! Pop! That was the end of the fleas.

**The boiler in the rubber mill**

I started work at Capen Heaton rubber mill. I was helping to make big rubber boxes for submarine batteries. At first I used to push trolley-loads of rubber into this huge steam-oven. I slammed the door, bolted it, turned on the steam, and cured the rubber to toughen it. All the steam had to be let out before I undid the bolts. I had a large stick with a hook on that I used to pull out the two steel trolleys. To reach the second one, I had to get right inside the oven, and by golly it was hot in there!

**Working on the presses**

Then I worked on the machines that pressed rubber into moulds to make covers for electrical connections.

They were powerful, dangerous things, those presses. Once one of the men was reaching into a press to get a newly pressed piece of rubber out. A fitter working nearby knocked a lever with his knee. The press started. I heard a scream. People rushed to help. The press had sliced off all the fingers of the man's hand.

Another man lost his hand, and a third had his arm cut off in the rolling mill. Only after accidents like that did they make the machines safe.

1986

F.S. Smith

# ARMY DAYS
## *Palestine, Corfu and*
## *Portsmouth*
## 1946–1953

### Scrubbing Private Johnson

In 1946 I joined the army. After some
training in Cornwall, I was posted to the Royal
West Kent regiment. We were in
Gravesend, waiting to set off for Egypt and
Palestine, when this happened.
We were parading for inspection. It was freezing
cold, snowing in fact. The Regimental
Sergeant Major noticed that Private Johnson had
dirt on his neck.
'Johnson! You're filthy! You, you and you' – he
pointed at me and two mates – 'take
Johnson inside and scrub the bastard down.'
Here we are doing as we are told,
watched by the RSM. There was no heating,
and we used cold water. I can't forget
Johnson shaking, his teeth chattering, and goose-
pimples all over him.

123

1989
F. S. Smith

**Forced march by the Dead Sea**

In 1947 we went to Palestine. It had been under British control since 1918. The Jews had been fighting to have their own country. Now Britain was pulling out. Palestine was going to be divided between Jews and Arabs. The Arabs were fighting the Jews to stop Israel being founded. We were in the middle.

For our endurance training, we went from Jerusalem by truck, then started a forced march through the desert to a campsite between Jordan and Palestine. I was carrying a Bren gun and ammunition. The heat was terrible. Twenty miles a day we covered, taking salt tablets to replace what we sweated out, with the lads complaining they couldn't go on.

In the end we made camp all right. I'm cleaning my Bren gun, just in case of an attack by Jews or Arabs – it could have been either, we had no idea.

**A Jewish armoured car** Near Jerusalem, some fifteen Jewish workers were ambushed and killed by about two hundred Arabs. We went there to clear up. We exchanged some fire with the Arabs, and killed some I believe, then carried the bodies back to the Jewish settlement. They gave us some tea, and we saw this armoured car, a lorry with metal plates to protect the Jews as they went out to work.

**A Jewish convoy**

Our job was to keep the roads open for British troops. We patrolled between the Gaza Strip and Jerusalem. Arabs and Jews also used the road. It was a risky business, because the Arabs often sniped from hilltops or made ambushes. The Jews didn't rely just on us – they made their own convoys, like this one on its way to Jerusalem.

The Arabs used to tell me they would push the Jews into the sea. There were more of them than the Jews, but I knew it wouldn't be that easy. More Jews were coming in all the time, and they would fight to the death for their country.

### The dying soldier

One day three of us went out in our truck to patrol our area. I was sitting over one wheel-arch, and opposite me was a private called Harris. We had just left camp when I heard a single shot. Private Harris shouted 'Mother!' and fell forward, right into my arms. He'd been hit. The bullet must have come from behind him, right towards me. If he hadn't been there, it would have been me lying there not him. I yelled to the driver, 'Get back to camp!' and laid him down on my arm. I felt dizzy and sick, which I put down to shock.

We tore into camp, horn blasting. I pulled out the pin holding the tail-board up, helped get Harris out and on to a stretcher, grabbed my Bren gun, and started walking. Suddenly I felt a shooting pain in my stomach. I stopped, my head spinning.

'Smith,' someone said, 'There's blood running down your trousers.'

Then I passed out.

I came round in the hospital. Harris had died. The bullet that killed him had gone right through him and into my stomach. With the shock of it all, I simply hadn't noticed. I was in hospital for a month. They operated, stitched me up and sent me out, back to my duties.

I thought it was all sorted out. It wasn't till thirty-eight years later, when I was bothered by some pains in my stomach, that I discovered the bullet was still in me. It's still there now, but it's not a problem any more.

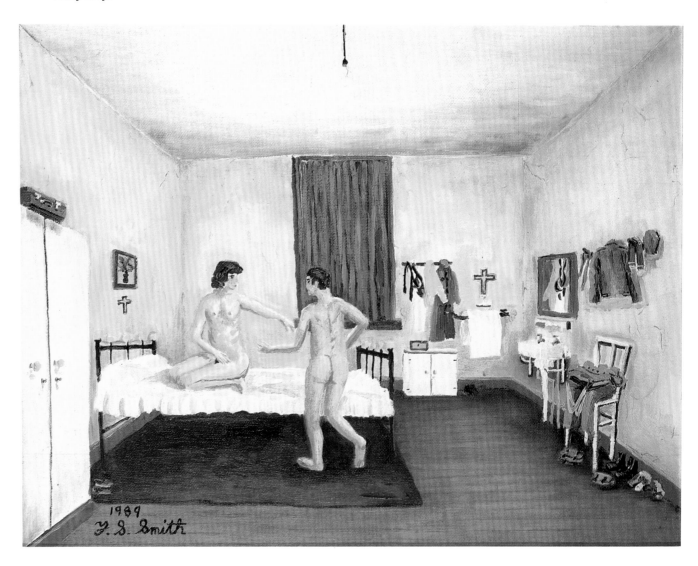

1989
Y. S. Smith

**Virgin soldier no more**

After Palestine, we were based in Athens. Once, on leave, we had a few drinks at a taverna – champagne, vodka, ouzo, all new to me. We were served by some ladies, who treated us very nicely.

One of them said to me, 'You come with me?'

'Show us your black book!' said one of the soldiers, who knew more about things than I did.

'Me see doctor many times,' she said indignantly. 'Me no VD.'

There was a burst of laughter from the others, and shouts of, 'Go on then, Frank!'

I knew she was a prostitute, but I didn't know exactly what to expect. I followed her to her room.

'Take off clothes,' she said, so I did. She made the sign of the cross in front of her crucifix, got on the bed, then she held out her hand to me.

She was a very strong, forceful girl. So it was soon over.

That was my first sexual experience. We got dressed, and I paid her.

Then we both went back to the taverna. The others cheered and laughed as we walked in, and someone shouted for more champagne.

### Final celebration in Corfu

For a year I was in Corfu, near the little fishing village of Hipsos, as an under-chef with the British Military Mission. We were in a villa which used to belong to the Italian royal family before the war. When the British invaded to drive the Germans out, the Royal Marines were based in it.

The Military Mission was part of MI5, so our work was secret. We had to sign the Official Secrets Act. There was a war in Greece with Communists, and the job of the MI5 officers was to send radio messages, mainly to agents in Albania when the British were trying to make sure Albania didn't go Communist. It was a disaster, because the agents were all picked up. I learned much later that was because the Communist spy Kim Philby had passed on information to the Russians about the landing sites.

I knew hardly anything about all this at the time, because we weren't allowed upstairs where the radio equipment was. I was with about ten other ordinary soldiers, just doing our work and enjoying ourselves. The sergeant spoke Greek, and he was our translator when we went out for a meal.

Once we were in real danger. A boatload of agents came from Albania to blow the villa up. It went off course in bad weather, and landed too far down the coast. There was a battle, and two were shot and the rest captured. After that, the villa closed down.

This picture is of our final celebration at the local taverna in Hipsos. I'm in the middle of the group, which is sitting at two tables, between two mates, Traherne and Dutton. Not all of us are there, because the others had guard duty.

F. S. Smith 1986

**Learning gunnery with the Royal Marines**

Wanting to get ahead, I volunteered for Korea, and also put in for a transfer to the Royal Marines. It meant going through a whole new training, but that was all right. After initial training, I started naval gunnery at Hasler Gunnery School, Portsmouth.

This is the training bridge of a six-inch gun, which was too large for the whole thing to be on site. A barrel six inches across is a pretty big barrel. Here we learned all the commands and actions, and all about shells and high explosives, and how to aim the gun.

1986
F.S. Smith

**The four-inch gun**    Here I am at the breech of a four-inch gun. The three others are the rest of the team it takes to work the gun and aim it. You had to get the elevation right, of course, but also the deflection, to allow for the target's movement.

1989
F.S.Smith

**The taverna owner**

I've always wanted to go back to Hipsos, so I painted this from a photograph to take with me as a present. It's of the taverna owner (he's second from the left) and his family. They were marvellous people, very generous to us, although they were very poor. I've even got a bronze plaque ready for them:

'Presented to the people of Hipsos, Corfu, from the artist Frank Sidney Smith in thanks for their kindness during 1949.'

**Commando training on Dartmoor**

Dartmoor is a rough wilderness for man and beast. Rain, fog, bogs, streams, mud – we were expected to cope with the lot. It was miserable dragging off wet clothes at night, and worse putting them back on still wet in the morning. Here we are out on manoeuvres, cooking for the others.

Then, in 1952, I was off to Korea on HMS Newcastle, protecting destroyers around the coast. I had my ear-drums damaged by the six-inch guns, which changed the course of my life.

Another important thing happened on active service: I saw a magazine advertisement from a girl who wanted a pen-friend. Her name was Doris, and I liked the way she described herself, so I blacked out the advertisement to make sure no one else wrote to her, and sent her a letter. She replied, and we began to exchange regular letters.

### Infantry training

The infantry training at Lympstone, between Exeter and Exmouth, was tough for some, but not for me after four years in the army. I didn't mind the corrugated iron huts, the drilling, route-marches and night manoeuvres. On the route-marches you always got the stragglers:

'I can't go on, Sergeant!'

'You bloody well can, and you will, Bennett, or this lot goes out and does the route all over again, and you go with them.'

So sometimes we ended the march carrying an extra rifle or an extra pack, while some poor bugger limped in beside me.

### The back-house

I was demobbed in 1953, being declared medically unfit because of the damage to my ears. While I was in hospital, Doris came to see me. We fell in love, and arranged to marry. But on the very day of the wedding she had a nervous breakdown and was put in hospital.

That was the start of her schizophrenia, though I didn't know anything about it then. At first, it seemed as if she would be OK, because she started on drugs which made her better.

I went back to Bournville and got a job with Austin's as a storeman. Doris joined me and we got married.

We lived in rooms at Mrs Ales's in Maryvale Road.

My older brother Reg, who had been in the army, got a council house with his new wife and their baby.

It wasn't much of a house. It was what they called a 'back-house', because it was one of a line of houses that was joined to another line of houses, back to back. It was a one-up, one-down, with a small kitchen about four feet square, sharing a toilet and wash-house. Their house looked over this yard, where you can see children playing and washing hanging out. It was a miserable place, so badly built the bed-legs once broke right through the floor, dumping plaster on to the baby's pram.

Not long after, they were all condemned.

# THE MAYPOLE

*Birmingham*

1953–1992

**The painted bath**

At Mrs Ales's, the bath was covered with rust spots. Once Mrs Ales thought she would make the bathroom look nicer by painting the bath. She told me not to use it for a week.

After a week I had a bath, nice hot water and plenty of soap. When I got out, I noticed these white footprints on the floor. My feet were white. Then I saw in the mirror my legs, bottom and back were all white too – wet paint.

Here's Doris cleaning me off with turpentine. Doris is laughing, but I'm furious – 'That stupid bloody woman!' – and that's making Doris laugh all the more.

Funny old thing, Mrs Ales was – every Thursday she would come to collect the rent, but she never came in, just stood outside the door and coughed until I paid her.

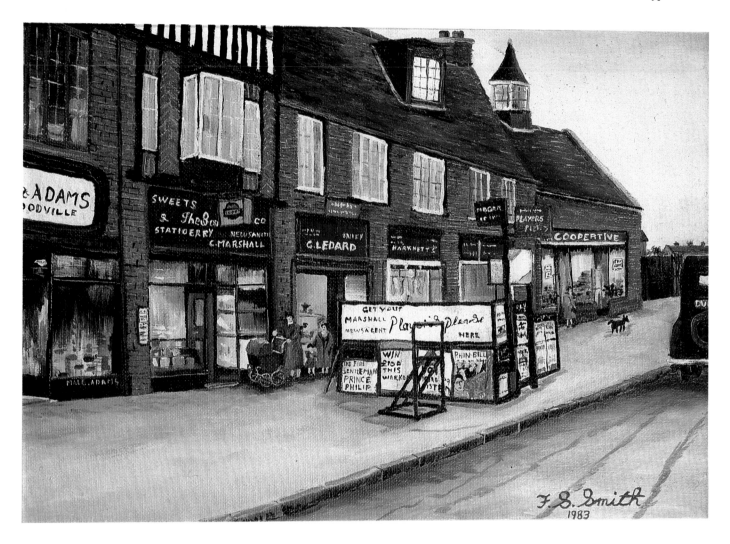

**The Maypole**

In 1954 Doris and I bought a house in The Maypole, Birmingham. We saved for a deposit, and also had some help from Doris's father. It was a lovely place then, like a village, still outside Birmingham itself, quiet with little family shops. There was even a blacksmith. The fields started at the end of our road.

I'm still in the same house, but things have changed a bit. The main road is a motorway, and most of the shops have become part of supermarkets.

139

### The Maypole cinema

The cinema was built in the late 1930s. When we moved in it was going strong. We went every week. It was always clean and nice. Then in the 1950s television took its toll, and it had to close.

This was its last show – *The Lost World* – with crowds of children and grown-ups queuing up for tickets.

Then they tried to use it for wrestling, and that was a flop. Then Brooms, the demolishers, moved in. Funnily enough, Brooms was run by a mother-and-daughter team. It was a sight, two women bashing away with fourteen-pound hammers. That was the end of the Maypole cinema. On the site is a supermarket now.

## Austin's

For twenty years I worked for Austin's, first at Longbridge, then at King's Norton, where they made their first automatic gearbox. This is the King's Norton factory. In the mid-1970s it was a really modern place, air-conditioned, clean, with an efficient assembly line that moved the components along on pendants. I liked it there, because I discovered an interest in factories as an artist. I often spent my breaks sketching.

Unfortunately, the factory didn't go on working. The site was rented, and when the rent went up the prices rose and sales dropped. I was afraid of being made redundant, but instead I got shifted to the Rover plant at Percy Road to work on Land Rover gearboxes.

PREPARE TO
MEET THY
GOD.
THE END OF THE
WORLD IS
NEAR.

### The eccentric prophet

The first time I saw this man I was so surprised I rode my bike on to the pavement and fell off. Then I noticed where he lived, and saw him many times. He had a white beard and white hair like a prophet, and his bicycle was protected in the front by half a dustbin. His house was full of junk and his front window was plastered with posters.

(*Opposite page*)

### The factory at Percy Road

Working in the factory that made Land Rover gearboxes was like going into the Dark Ages it was so old-fashioned.

But for me that was good. All that detail! I could have drawn for a year non-stop. I've painted myself here on the factory floor, by a stack of gearbox housings.

1985

F. S. Smith

**My new tool**

My job was putting the studs into gearbox housings. At first I had to do it by hand. The housings were balanced on tins and were tied on to the benches with string. I'm using an airgun to fix the bolts, but it took me four years of asking to get it. On the left is a press that pushes the bearings into the housings. In the background is the washer for cleaning the housings before work started on them.

**Cleaning the bolts**

This place was so smelly, dirty, noisy and antiquated that I had to paint it. It was an industrial relic.

It was run by a Jamaican, a nice man who worked hard. He is holding a box of greasy new bolts, which he is about to take to the chemical tank at the back to be washed. That's where the smell comes from. Then they go through a drier. Finally, they're blackened and put on to the conveyer belt on the right, ready to be put into the gearboxes.

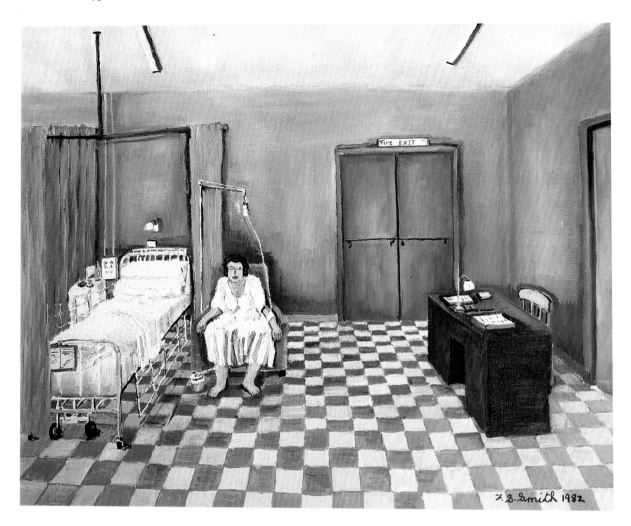

F.S.Smith 1982

### My wife's death

All this while, Doris had been suffering on and off with schizophrenia. When she was well she was the best wife and mother, and I loved her deeply. But often she was in hospital. Those times, I had been looking after our two boys, Roger and Gregory. The neighbours and my two brothers helped a lot, because I also had to work in the factory.

In 1979 she went into hospital again. She seemed to be slipping away into a coma. It was depressing seeing her. She sat there on a drip, hardly able to recognize her husband and sons. No one explained why, or what the treatment was.

One night at twelve-thirty the doorbell rang. It was the police. 'Mr Smith, would you phone the hospital?' We didn't have a phone. I well remember standing in the phone booth and hearing the nurse say they were sorry, but my wife had died. I went home, and the two boys and I broke down, crying.

The hospital gave me a letter to take to the Registrar of Deaths. There they told me what the letter said: the cause of death was lithium poisoning. Later, the coroner stated it was death by misadventure.

That was a terrible thing to learn, and it made me angry. I took legal action and the case went on for years. Eventually, after nine years, the hospital settled out of court. £1600 they paid. But how could they make up for a life lost? And how could they make up for the effect of Doris's death on Roger?

## Resting at dinner time

Since I didn't get much sleep at night, I often took a nap during my breaks at work. Here I am in my corner.

I slept deeply during the breaks. The others sometimes played tricks on me. Once they tied my boots together. When I woke up, I stood up and fell over. Another time when I was snoring, someone dropped a tin just by me, making me jump out of my skin.

Soon after Doris's death I was made redundant because the place was too noisy. I had been sensitive to noise ever since the naval guns damaged my ear-drums.

Not long after the Percy Road works were bulldozed. It's all flat concrete now.

F. Smith 1981

## Trouble with Roger

In his mid-twenties, Roger developed this craze for citizens' band radio. Here he is in his flying jacket, calling up mates. His code name was 'Coughing Dogger', I never knew why. I could hardly understand him when he talked – it was all slang. For a while I was happy to leave him alone. That was what he wanted, and I was busy finishing an extension which I'd started before Doris died. The only thing I knew was that he was for ever making dates, mostly with girls, most of them teenagers, sometimes with men.

His behaviour started to change. He started to drink a lot. He brought rough friends home. I discovered he was taking drugs, and then found out he was hanging around with drug-pushers. I realized he was unstable, like his mother. There were many rows, and many tears. Sometimes he was violent.

**Watching the pushers**

Roger used to meet men in the local pub. I was so determined not to let him get deeper into crime, depression and violence that I decided to set the police on to his drug-pushing mates. I started to visit the pub, and watched them. I remembered everything I saw and made little sketches at home that eventually helped the police to pick up a few of the men.

I watched that pub go steadily downhill. Anything there was fair game. The ornaments were stuck to the wall, but they still got stolen. Once, I saw this – two men hauling away a Space Invaders machine, while the crowd just looked on.

No one paid me any attention. By then I was a regular, and they trusted me not to say anything.

Later, one of the thieves told me they had taken the cash out of the machine and sold it. 'Eight hundred quid, all told. Not bad, eh, Frank?'

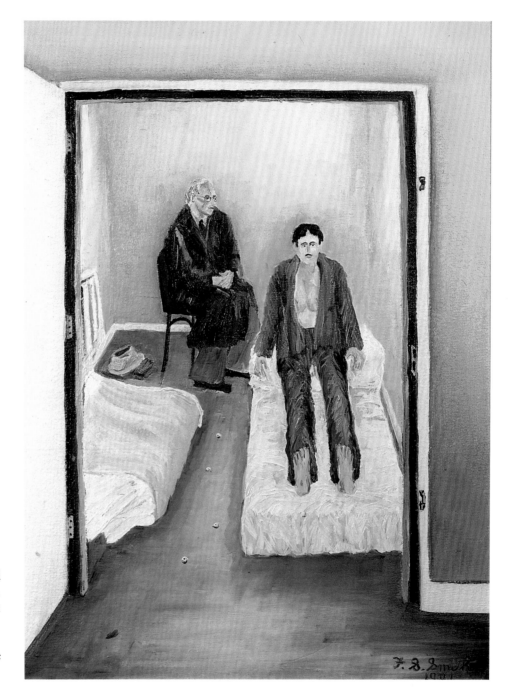

### Roger in hospital

Eventually Roger got so bad I had to send for the doctor. Roger was taken to the mental hospital, the same one Doris had been in.

Next time I saw him he was in this special room, almost like a padded cell, with the light concealed so there was no risk of suicide with the flex. Like his mother he was on drugs now, not lithium but largactil. It was to control his violence. Once he was so violent he tore the lavatory bowl right off its concrete stand. He also had shock treatment. He would cry, and so would I, as he begged to be taken home. It was not good for him to be in there, but I knew it would be worse at home, where I couldn't control him and he would be back with his drug-pushing friends.

## My son is now at rest

Roger seemed to respond to his treatment enough to be allowed out. On one trip he got knocked over and was unconscious for two hours. That seemed to change him again. He became very quiet and depressed, not like before. But at least he was not violent, and was well enough to come home to his flat on the sixth floor of a new block. He even started work.

One day in November 1988 a policeman came to my house, telling me I had better get to the hospital. Roger had fallen from his flat, but the policeman couldn't tell me anything else.

At the hospital a sister took me to a room and closed the door.

'Mr Smith, I'm sorry to have to tell you your son is dead.'

The shock of it. It felt as if it was me that had fallen.

Just then Gregory came in. I told him what had happened. He shouted 'No! No!' and we both cried.

Then I had to identify Roger. When I saw him, tears poured down my cheeks.

'Yes,' I said. 'That's my son, Roger.'

I kissed him on the cheek, and said 'Well, son, you're at rest at last.' Those were my last words to him. He was a kind and loving boy.

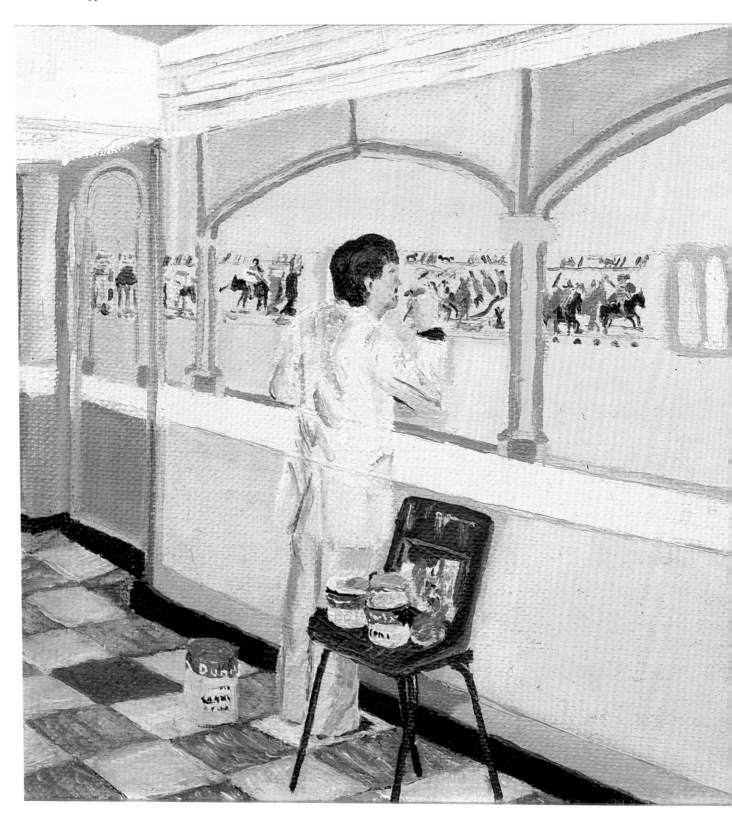

S. Smith 1984

## Decorating the hospital

That hospital was a depressing place to visit, going in down the long, dark corridor. I should know, after all the years I came to visit Doris and Roger – the shouts and cries, the banging doors, the empty looks, the crazy singing.

But while Roger was in there students repainted the corridor. They copied an old tapestry. I took photographs so that I could get it right in this picture. It was a wonderful change, and it cheered up the patients and visitors. The patients damaged many things, but they never touched the painting in the corridor.

# EPILOGUE:
# RETURN TO THE
# WORKHOUSE

## Checking the records

When I started to paint my life, I had to go back to Minster to make sure I got the details right. Mother had not told me I was actually born in the workhouse until quite late on. She was embarrassed about it, and so was I.

In 1976 I went back to what was now Minster Hospital. I saw the buildings, and I remembered my childhood, and it brought tears to my eyes. I stood there, crying and speechless.

Then I went in, asked to speak to the person in charge and said I wanted to make some sketches.

'You say you were born here?'

'That's what my Mother said.'

'Would you like to see?'

He led me to this room which contained the register. There it was: Frank Sidney Smith, born 22 April 1928, christened in that very chapel.

Suddenly I knew there was no need to feel embarrassed. Instead I felt proud, and knew there was work to be done, recording all those buildings which had sheltered so many destitute mothers and unemployed men and poor children without proper families.

## The end of the workhouse

It was lucky I went back when I did, because soon after that the buildings were demolished. By then they knew me well enough to invite me along to watch. I saw little things scattered about on the ground that brought back memories – an old Bible, a laundry book, a small clock, some coal from the boilerhouse. People came from all over Kent to watch the past fall down. Last to go was this chimney. Down went the plunger, the cameras clicked, and that was the end of the boilerhouse chimney.

## Night class

I began going to art classes in 1976. I was
painting from calendars, but I realized it
was no good copying other people's work.
So I told Doris and the boys I wanted to
paint my life. I was the odd one out, standing
up at an easel painting in oils when most of
the others sat and used watercolours. There
I am, painting scenes from my life when
everyone else is doing still-lifes and
landscapes. The picture is *The Painted Bath*
(p. 138).

Doris and the boys thought I was mad.
In fact I think it was the one thing that kept
me sane. I think I really would have gone
mad with the strain of what happened to
Doris and Roger if I hadn't had the art class.

I still go, because there's still so much to
do. This book is only a beginning.

## Acknowledgements

I would like to thank the following:

all the night-school teachers for the help
they have given me over the years, especially
Janet Malloy, Jackie Furmston, Janet Emery,
and Jane Ellis; all the voluntary helpers who
came to help us with our writing; Graham
Blaine, my art teacher; my art student
friends; George Holmes, always good for a
laugh; the staff in the office, for their happy
smiles whenever I pop in to see them; the
head teacher, Mike Sprawson; and Jean Rose
and Christine Holloway who were kind
enough to type my writing out for me;

the people of Tanworth-in-Arden, who did
so much for me when I was a boy there in
the war;

the house-mothers and house-fathers in Kent
who did so much to help the children in the
Manston Homes;

RAF Manston for their kindness to the
Manston Homes children;

John Village, a life-long friend until his death
in 1991. We spent many happy days
painting together in the countryside;

Dora Bagnall, who helped look after the
children when Doris was ill;

Kathleen Dayus and David Olliver for their
interest

Geoffrey Goode, for photographing my
pictures;

everyone who has worked to make a success
of the book at Weidenfeld & Nicolson;

John Man, for helping me with this book;

all my friends who helped with the research
for the paintings. Without them, this book
could not have been done.

F. S. Smith
*King's Heath, Birmingham*
February 1993